FROM GASLIGHTING TO TRUTHLIGHTING

A NEW FRAMEWORK FOR ADVANCING FAIR OPPORTUNITIES FOR WOMEN IN THE WORKPLACE

DR. FALGUNI SHAH

ISBN: 979-8-9993943-0-9 (hardcover)
ISBN: 979-8-9993943-1-6 (paperback)
ISBN: 979-8-9993943-2-3 (ebook)

Publishing Company: Golden Grit Press

CONTENTS

PART III – ADVANCING FAIR OPPORTUNITIES

FOREWORD

Dr. Falguni Shah's *From Gaslighting to Truthlighting* emerges as a pivotal text at a time when diversity, equity, and inclusion practices and practitioners in corporate America are under attack. As a friend and colleague who has witnessed Falguni's tireless dedication to equity firsthand, I am deeply moved by her work's critical importance and timeliness. Her passion for advocating real change is not just inspiring; it's a vital force driving the conversation around diversity, equity, and inclusion forward in times when it's most needed. This book transcends a mere analysis of the obstacles encountered by minority women; it is a manifesto for substantial change, a detailed scholarly study, and an intimate narrative intertwined with the collective experiences of many.

In Falguni's book, the pervasive issues of inequity within corporate America are laid bare. Her work exposes significant salary and career advancement disparities, particularly affecting minority women, where deep-seated racial and gender biases undercut the claims of equal opportunity by Fortune

500 companies. The book scrutinizes a biased promotion system that favors candidates who align with the personal and demographic preferences of decision-makers, thereby perpetuating a cycle of subjective bias. Falguni discusses the substantial challenges of cultural isolation that minority women face, significantly hindering their ability to build essential networks for career advancement. Together, these elements depict a corporate environment where systemic changes are crucial for fostering genuine equity and inclusion.

Throughout my career as a leader in diversity talent acquisition and development, I have witnessed the systematic obstacles and racism that Falguni describes. The familiar patterns of favoritism and in-group bias, particularly prevalent in promotion practices within corporate settings, underscore the need for the strategies Falguni advocates.

Falguni introduces the Fair-Opportunity Framework, a comprehensive six-step plan to dismantle inequities within promotional systems. This framework begins with an in-depth audit of current processes to pinpoint biases and inconsistencies. It stresses establishing clear, collaboratively developed promotion criteria, transparency in decision-making, and regular monitoring outcomes to adjust policies effectively. It also emphasizes ongoing training for decision-makers to recognize and mitigate unconscious biases and calls for open communication channels, including regular town halls and feedback mechanisms to build trust among staff.

To truly embrace the spirit of transparency and fairness that Falguni champions, one must understand and implement her innovative concept of "truthlighting." This approach serves as a powerful tool to illuminate the often-overlooked truths within corporate environments, ensuring that every voice is heard and valued. This method serves as an antithesis to traditional practices that often resemble gaslighting—where individual experiences are diminished and manipulation is perpetuated. Truthlighting shines a light on truths, validates experiences, and highlights the accomplishments of those marginalized by systemic biases, ensuring that every voice is heard and valued.

Integrating truthlighting into the Fair-Opportunity Framework creates a holistic model that identifies and removes barriers and proactively reinforces equity principles through clear, data-driven transparency and robust accountability measures. For example, when biases in promotion decisions are raised, the truthlighting approach addresses these concerns directly with detailed data and structured review processes that are documented and accessible to all stakeholders.

From Gaslighting to Truthlighting goes beyond critiquing to offer a revolutionary perspective on how organizations operate, challenging leaders to reform their practices actively and create genuinely equitable advancement pathways. Falguni's work encourages a shift from passive acknowledgment of diversity to active engagement with inclusion and equity.

As you delve into *From Gaslighting to Truthlighting*, let it inspire action and serve as a guide through the complexities of institutional reform. Inspired by the resilient spirit of figures like Sona, Falguni's great-grandmother, who defied oppressive norms to enlighten and empower others, we, too, are called to dismantle the modern barriers that restrict many in our workplaces.

This book is more than just a read; it is a call to action—a blueprint for building workplaces where every employee is valued for their uniqueness and undeniable potential. These stories and the book's frameworks provide readers—whether they are executives, managers, or HR professionals—with the tools needed to foster a more just corporate environment. It is an indispensable resource for anyone committed to real change, providing insights and a strategic framework adaptable to any organization's unique challenges and opportunities.

As you turn these pages, I invite you to engage deeply with the material, reflect on your practices, and consider how you might contribute to creating equitable pathways for all employees in your sphere of influence. Let us take inspiration from Falguni's great-grandmother, Sona, who defied the norms of her time and paved the way for future generations. Like Sona, let us all be trailblazers in our right, advocating for equity and justice with courage and determination.

Riikka Salonen, MA
Managing Director, Health Equity and Global
Diversity, Equity, and Inclusion
BCT Partners, LLC

ENDORSEMENTS

"This book is an indispensable resource for anyone committed to advancing diversity and inclusion in corporate environments. By sharing women's firsthand experiences in their quest for promotion, Shah unveils both the obstacles they face and the successful strategies that have propelled them forward. This book is an important resource for HR teams, managers, and employees."

—Deepa Purushothaman, Author of
The First, The Few, The Only

"Falguni Shah's: *From Gaslighting to Truthlighting* is an informative, illuminating, and insightful foray into the realities minority women face in corporate America. This timely and important book offers an artful combination of powerful stories, practical tools, and proven strategies, all supported by research. It is an invaluable resource for minority women and the supervisors, mentors, sponsors, and allies who aspire to be equal partners in their success."

—Dr. Randal Pinkett, Chairman and CEO of
BCT Partners and Award-winning Author of
Data-Driven DEI and *Black Faces in High Places*

"I applaud this book *From Gaslighting to Truthlighting* for its emphasis on the importance of self-promotion for women in corporate positions. Too often, women are taught to downplay their achievements, but this book encourages them to advocate for themselves boldly. By providing practical tools and tips, Dr. Shah provides a roadmap for truthlighting that will empower women to showcase their talents and expertise effectively, ultimately paving the way for their greater success in the workplace."

—Dr Niru Kumar, Founder and CEO of
Ask Insight and Padma Shri, 2021

Falguni Shah's book is a must-have for professionals in all industries and fields. This thoughtful and thought-provoking work provides insight into the often-overlooked experience of minority women, making it an invaluable read for leaders, HR and Inclusion professionals, mentors, women starting their career journeys, and everyone else in between. Falguni has used her own research to fuel this book, showcasing her subject matter expertise, extensive experience, and critical thinking skills to provide real-world strategies that can have a lasting and significant impact.

—Dr. Marianne Cabrera, Program Director of
Organizational Leadership Degree Programs,
Adler University

INTRODUCING TRUTHLIGHTING

Truthlighting: Shining a Light on Truth in the Workplace

GASLIGHTING IS A form of psychological manipulation where a person or a group makes someone question their reality, memory, or perception. It often involves denial, misdirection, contradiction, or lying to make the victim feel confused, doubtful of their experiences, or even mentally unstable.

For example, if someone clearly remembers an event happening, but another person insists it never did—despite evidence—this could be gaslighting. It commonly occurs in relationships where one person wants to control and undermine the other.

Truthlighting is the opposite of gaslighting. While gaslighting distorts reality, making individuals doubt their experiences and perceptions, truthlighting illuminates the truth, affirms reality instead of distorting it, and reinforces trust rather than manipulation and deception.

In the workplace, gaslighting can take the form of dismissing concerns about bias, denying unequal treatment, or making employees feel like their struggles are imagined. Truthlighting, by contrast, is an intentional effort to bring transparency, honesty, and accountability to workplace interactions, particularly in hiring, promotions, and leadership development.

Key Aspects of Truthlighting

❯ Acknowledging Bias Instead of Denying It

Gaslighting response: You didn't get the promotion because you're not ready yet (without providing clear reasoning or criteria). You did not get the promotion because you are applying for any promotion that offers more money. This is clearly eroding confidence and self-trust.

Truthlighting response: Here are the exact criteria for promotion and the areas where you can strengthen your skills to be considered next time. Be mindful of any affinity and/or familiarity bias in decision-making by implementing consensus-based decision-making with a diverse hiring panel. Individuals can feel secure in their judgments and decisions.

❯ Engaging in Fair Opportunity

Gaslighting response: We will open the position for everyone in the team to provide equal opportunity, but XYZ individuals are already performing at this level (implying they will get preference). Here, they use misinformation to confuse others and distort reality or intention.

Truthlighting response: Communicate the role's requirements, open the position for all, and provide fair interviews. They provide clear communication and leadership accountability to follow a standardized process for posting positions and interviewing.

▶ Providing Data-Driven Transparency

Gaslighting response: We need to fill the position immediately. You are going on maternity leave shortly. Everyone has an equal shot at leadership roles (while promotion data shows clear disparities).

Truthlighting response: Here's our company's promotion data broken down by demographics, and here's what we're doing to ensure a fairer process.

▶ Validating Lived Experiences

Gaslighting response: You're being too sensitive. No one is treated unfairly here. When the employee provides critical feedback about a situation when another colleague refused to work with them, the manager doubles down on the employee and says, "If you want to develop your leadership skills, you will need to have crucial conversations." This is creating a toxic and distrustful environment.

Truthlighting response: I hear your concerns. Let's examine the patterns and discuss how we can improve fairness in the process. This will build a culture where employees can speak up without fear of being dismissed or manipulated.

▶ Encouraging Open Dialogue and Accountability

Gaslighting response: Someone is hired two levels below their current capacity and made to work toward a promotion in the future. That's just how the system works. You need to work harder.

Truthlighting response: Let's examine our system and identify if structural barriers need to be addressed.

Why Truthlighting Matters

Truthlighting fosters psychological safety, allowing employees—especially those from underrepresented groups—to express concerns, seek support, and advocate for fair treatment without fear of being dismissed. It builds trust and credibility within organizations by ensuring transparency in decision-making and providing employees with clear, actionable pathways for growth.

By adopting truthlighting as a workplace practice, leaders, managers, and HR professionals can actively work toward equity and inclusion, creating environments where all employees feel valued, respected, and empowered to succeed. The act of truthlighting shines a spotlight on employees' achievements and advocates for their growth.

Leaders practicing truthlighting openly acknowledge concerns, validate employees' perspectives, communicate transparently, and create a safe environment. HR policies reflect integrity, ensuring feedback and evaluations are based on facts rather than manipulation. Team discussions encourage truth-seeking and constructive dialogue rather than gaslighting behaviors like blame-shifting. Truthlighting is about fostering a workplace culture where truth, clarity, and trust are prioritized over manipulation and doubt.

A PERSONAL CALLING

WHILE MOST FORTUNE 500 companies consider themselves equal-opportunity employers, women continue to get significantly lower salaries than their male counterparts. Minority women continue to be at a disadvantage because of their race and ethnicity and face inequities and discrimination in the workplace. Moreover, existing research shows subjective bias in the performance appraisal process and inequities in merit-based promotion decisions. This book highlights the perceptions of minority women as they relate to internal workplace promotions and succession planning. It brings forward the realities of women in mid-level management in corporate America and their struggles to fulfill their career aspirations and individual growth. It provides a glimpse of their career progression journeys as they navigate corporate bureaucracies and inequities. Their stories reveal their successes and failures, what worked and what didn't, who helped them through this journey, and what steps they took to be successful. The hope is to enhance managers' awareness of challenges faced by minority women and provide necessary support and advocacy to reduce the barriers. The stories provide insight for women to examine their perceptions and obtain practical tools and tips on advancing in the workplace.

Familiarity Breeds Bias

Research shows that promotion is often biased because it depends on personal connections instead of merit. Managers tend to promote employees who are part of the in-group, who idealize them as managers, and who are their so-called "favorites."[1,2] Managers form initial impressions concerning the suitability of candidates for promotion based mainly on the candidates' personalities.[3] Decision-makers favor candidates of their gender or ethnicity and may have preconceived ideas about their attributes based on their demographics, which influences promotion decisions.[4] This system places an additional burden on those who do not begin as part of their in-group, including minorities and women.

Hence, minority leaders often find themselves isolated and struggle to network and build relationships due to cultural differences. To make the promotion process fair, the author provides an actionable framework for human resource (HR) teams, managers, and employees to reduce bias and increase promotability in the workplace.

Forged in Fire: The Making of Gold

The felt experience of injustice urges people to share their stories to connect with others with similar experiences to build a sense of support and community. This becomes a strong driver for people to come together and challenge the status quo. I am inspired, in part, to write this book by the courage of my great-grandmother, Sona, who made bold moves to challenge the norms and barriers faced by women in India in the 1900s.

My great-grandmother was born on July 23, 1906, with the appropriate name of Sona, which means gold, a precious metal created by nuclear fusion, high energy, heat, and pressure. As her name suggests, she turned out to be as precious as gold for truth seekers, especially women, for generations to come. Sona was born into a religious Hindu family in a small village in Gujarat, India. It was a predominantly male-dominated society that restrained women to the limited duties of a mother, wife, and daughter. At an early age, she had a strong inclination toward spirituality. However, she had to follow the norms set by society; one such custom was child marriage. She was married at thirteen to her sister's husband, who was thirty-six, to care for her children after she passed. After the wedding, Sona sincerely served her family. She won the hearts of everyone as she nurtured the kids and remained friendly and helpful to all the villagers and neighbors. A few years later, her husband died.

Despite her loss, Sona was not shaken. She did not shed a single tear and remained positive by thinking that her childhood and married life were meant to be short. Now, she could entirely devote herself to spirituality without family obligations. Respecting the societal customs practiced by widows in those times, she shaved her head and refrained from wearing ornate clothes or jewelry. Several unrelated men offered to help her manage her financial accounts and household chores, but she disregarded those offers. While continuing her spiritual endeavors, she wholeheartedly accepted the dual role of being a mother and father for her young children. She single-handedly faced these odds.

▶ Trailblazer: Defying Odds

In the 1900s, societal norms restricted women, as they were not considered equal to men. There was a preference for married couples to have male children. Educational opportunities for women were more available in urban India. Opportunities and resources were limited in the remote villages and small towns versus metropolitan urban cities. The village where Sona grew up had one school, and it was only for boys. However, when her brother got ready for school, Sona also got ready. She wanted to study, so she accompanied her brother to school, even though she was the only girl there. As Sona accompanied her brother to the village school each day, she felt a mixture of excitement and trepidation. The dusty pathways lined with huts and fields whispered stories of tradition and limitation. Yet, in her heart, Sona carried an unwavering determination to defy the norms of her time. Inside the modest schoolhouse, Sona's presence stirred whispers among the boys. Some giggled, others cast curious glances, but Sona paid them no mind. She was there for a purpose—to quench her thirst for knowledge and to carve a path where none existed before. The schoolmaster, a stern-faced man with a graying beard, eyed her skeptically. "What business does a girl have in a place like this?" he grumbled, his voice a rumble of disapproval. Undeterred, Sona squared her shoulders and met his gaze head-on. "I am here to learn, just like my brother," she declared with quiet resolve.

Despite the initial resistance, Sona's determination soon won over the schoolmaster. He relented, allowing her to stay under one condition: She proved herself worthy of the education she sought. And prove herself she did. Sona immersed herself in her studies with fervor, devouring every lesson with an insatiable hunger for knowledge. She pored over textbooks and scratched diligently at her writing slate, determined to excel despite the odds stacked against her. As Sona delved deeper into her studies, she was drawn to the world of numbers and letters like a moth to a flame. With each passing day, her understanding of arithmetic and language grew, and soon, she was solving equations and crafting sentences with a fluency that belied her young age. Her teachers marveled at her intelligence, praising her quick grasp of concepts and insatiable thirst for knowledge. Sona's presence became a familiar sight in the village school. Once wary of her intrusion, her classmates grew to respect her diligence and determination. She became a beacon of hope for girls across the village, inspiring them to defy expectations and pursue their dreams with courage and conviction. Slowly but surely, Sona began dismantling the barriers of gender inequality that had confined her and countless others.

▶ Legacy Redefined: My Daughters Will Not Shave Their Heads

When Sona's daughters came of marriage age, they had white spots on their skin, which were medically called Vitiligo. Due to a lack of education and deep-rooted superstition, in several parts of India, Vitiligo carries social stigma. It was considered highly contagious and a punishment for past sins. For her daughters, being married was considered the socially stable path, and having Vitiligo led to challenges in getting a suitable boy for marriage. Also, given Sona's inclination towards spirituality, her daughters decided they wanted to worship God and did not want to get married. When her daughters desired to lead unmarried and dedicated lives, she supported them and said, "There is nothing wrong with them remaining unwed and devoting to God." Socially, this was considered highly unusual since living a spiritual life would mean remaining sequestered from society. However, with

Sona's support, her daughters continued to live in regular society. Inspired by them, several other women also wanted to live similarly dedicated lives. They considered Sona and her daughters' lives as the ones with elevated understanding. They realized that to progress on the path of renunciation, it was important to have support from spiritual leaders (gurus), society, and an institution that supported their mental, physical, and spiritual needs. They considered Sona their guru, and the group continued to grow, ultimately with educated and other married women joining her.

As Sona continued to help dedicated women lead spiritual lives, an issue arose regarding whether the unmarried women should shave their heads, which was the custom followed for renunciants and widowed women in India at the time. In those days in India, there were only male barbers, so if a dedicated woman living a celibate life wanted to shave her head, she would have to allow a male barber to touch her. This would be considered highly inappropriate. For those dedicated women who were mothers, raising their children was still their responsibility. If the mother chose to be a renunciant (nun), the children would fear her shaved head. For all women, it would be uncomfortable to participate in necessary social activities with a shaved head, and it would be hard to distinguish them from widowed women.

Furthermore, educated women with professional jobs would not be able to hold their jobs with a shaved head. Sona explained, "These women and I have not chosen this path because we are social outcasts, because we have been rejected by society, or because we need security. We have chosen this path with full awareness and understanding in the pursuit of a goal greater than all material ideals." Dedicated women should be able to utilize their skills and education for their spiritual upliftment and the good of society. It would be a massive loss if they were confined to four walls.

Trustees/leaders of the temple and elderly respected devotees insisted that the women should shave their heads. They assumed that Sona would agree with them since she was more conservative. But Sona firmly replied, "All these dedicated women are like my daughters, and I am their mother. I can provide them with shelter, clothing, and food. I will not make them shave their heads for accommodations or two morsels of food. I do not want them to be simple renunciants. I want them to walk the highest paths of spirituality and lead others along that path. I want to offer the light of their faith and knowledge at the lotus feet of God!"

One of the senior devotees derided her, "You are advocating so much for these women. Are you also planning to dress and grow your hair like them? What is your motive? Do you still have some desires left?"

Sona realized that she would have to tolerate and respond to such ignorance with positive clarification to bring about a change and create open acceptance. She could not remain aloof and make a positive impact on society. She replied with a calm demeanor and a soft tone, "I have lived my life to the fullest. Now, these remaining years are a gift from my guru. I do not have a personal agenda. I am living solely for my spiritual upliftment and my guru's mission. I have completely surrendered to him and am not concerned about how I look—nor am I doing this to fulfill my ego. Whatever was once mine has been taken away. Now my 'I'-ness (ego) has dissolved, and I belong to everybody. The only thing I can call mine is this rosary." The profound words of this divine mother struck the devotees. After that, people started calling her Sonaba. (Ba means a divine mother.)

On June 21, 1965, a foundation stone was laid for a formal spiritual organization named Gunatit Jyot[5] (meaning a beacon of light and named after her daughter Jyoti), the residence building for the new establishment for women, and the temple to be built next to it. On June 1, 1966, fifty-one dedicated women took formal initiation into sainthood. By 1980, the number had grown to 178. Today, there are over 500 ladies with branches around the world. These women demonstrate illustrious spiritual qualities and are beacons for the societies they serve and participate in. Sonaba moved to Gunatit Jyot from her home in Mumbai as soon as the construction was complete. This became her new home, and she would live there, giving her maternal love and support to the dedicated women of Gunatit Jyot and the members of the other wings of the institution. Her love was unconditional, divine, and an unending fountain from which the new group would drink and draw strength. She had passed every trial and tribulation of her life with flying colors, always maintaining focus on God. With the Gunatit Jyot finally established, she spent the rest of her life in the service of devotees. While Sonaba left her physical body on January 21, 1995, her spirit remains eternal in the hearts of devotees and wherever women yearn to lead a life of saintliness in dedication to God.

Leading by Example: Insights from Sona's Journey

Reflecting on Sona's story and her courage, resilience, and unwavering commitment to progress laid the groundwork for the expansive freedoms and liberties enjoyed by not just women in her family, including me, but many others who came into her company. Each small victory and hard-fought gain represented a triumph over the entrenched norms and societal barriers that once confined women to narrow roles and limited possibilities. From securing the right to education to gaining recognition as an autonomous individual with agency and rights, every milestone marked a seismic shift in the landscape of gender equality. While I have highlighted a few incidences from her life, several other monumental changes were instituted based on Sona's thoughts and actions. She served as a beacon of hope, illuminating the way forward and inspiring future generations to continue the fight for equality.

As I reflect on my great-grandmother's struggles and triumphs, I recognize the debt of gratitude I owe to her and other pioneering women in my ancestry. Their legacy lives on in the freedoms I cherish today, a testament to the enduring power of determination, perseverance, and collective action in pursuing a more just and equitable world. I hope my work on shining a light on corporate gender bias in the promotion and rewards process is a small repayment of that debt.

Sona's life exemplifies a visionary and transformational leader; I draw on her inspiration frequently. She inspired change and kept up with the changing times while remaining open to new and creative ideas that allowed many to live their aspirations. Today, her legacy remains alive and thriving, which shows sustainability. This is a story of not just her but of women who go through adversity and emerge as a hero. Speaking up and challenging the status quo requires courage. Challenging the norms and stereotypes that cause systemic injustice is like going against the water current. You need a boat with strong propellers, a strong backbone, and a passion to do that. Sona had the privilege and collective support to make this possible for the future generation. Her story inspires me to create new pathways for women and continue the legacy. Much like Sona many women who share this pressure to prove themselves can get the inspiration from her story to persevere.

Echoes of Purpose: Embracing My Calling

Growing up in India and being a woman, even though my family was supportive of my educational goals, there were several occasions where I was told that my education was to get a good husband. I had told myself, "I am going to be independent from the shackles of patriarchy. I refused to limit my role to marrying, bearing children, and being a homemaker." After my education in India, I decided to pursue further education and career development by moving to the United States. None of the girls from my family had ever moved out of the city for education, let alone out of the country. My family was worried; this was the first time I stood against them for my wishes and dreams. After much convincing and remaining firm in my goals, I immigrated to the United States from Mumbai, India, in 2001. I came to Chicago because I had family friends, an Indian community, and spiritual support. I lived independently for two years and finished my master's in community counseling at Loyola University, Chicago. I then started working at an Asian-owned non-profit community mental health agency in north Chicago, primarily serving immigrants, refugees, and low-income individuals with multiple comorbidities. This job was gratifying because I went through some of the challenges I helped others with. I was fortunate to have mentors who provided me with the support and resources to keep growing personally and professionally. Even though I had support from several leaders, I noticed subtle signs of push back against my progress, especially from men in leadership roles. There was pressure to prove myself in a predominantly white culture. It was a woman CEO at the time who believed in me, convinced the board, and promoted me to a manager role. This was my first time in a leadership role, and I excelled and grew very quickly.

Imposter's Ambition: Harnessing Doubt to Fuel Success

The pressure of "imposter syndrome" became the driving factor for success. Because of my relationship-building skills and expertise, I kept being offered new roles and rehired for specific skills for the position. I was respected and instrumental in creating new models of care, bringing increased revenue and growth. Like my great-grandmother, I also had a drive for change, an inclination to take on challenges, and a penchant for problem-solving. With my divergent thinking and growth mindset, I continued to excel in my career. I continued to move up the ladder until, one day, I could not convey my intentions. Leaders started seeing me as an opportunist (would take any position with a higher grade) and hungry for money when I expressed my desire for a promotion. I could not build trust with leadership despite being rated above and beyond every year, taking on new opportunities, putting myself in uncomfortable situations, and building new skills. Partly, it was because my team had a very rapid leadership turnover. I felt my intentions were misconstrued for the first time, and I couldn't develop trust with leadership. Until then, I had leaders who believed in me, recognized my talent, and guided me to attain greater heights. Something was drastically different. It was a company with predominantly white men in leadership and a very top-down culture where challenging the status quo was frowned upon. Creative ideas were ignored or did not register until later when the same idea was adopted or even stolen, and credit was not given where it was due. I continued to learn new skills and engage in professional development opportunities. Still, I felt like my flight at 3,000 miles per hour had crashed because of zero fuel, zero navigation support, and intentionally planted obstacles on the way. I started looking for support and validation from others I thought were in the same boat. I needed someone in a higher position of power in the hierarchy to lift my spirits, and I had to navigate out of this situation on my own.

In the following chapters, I will share the stories of women I interviewed that will echo my corporate experience and embody the same perseverance and resilience my great-grand-mother had. These women remind me daily to keep pursuing my dreams and turn self-doubt into self-confidence. We must change our narrative to turn imposter syndrome into imposter's ambition.

Beneath the Facade: Unveiling Injustice in Diversity, Equity, and Inclusion

In the realm of diversity, equity, and inclusion, the stated goal is to create equitable opportunities for advancement. However, in practice, these opportunities often fall short. Frequently, positions are ostensibly opened to provide equal chances for promotion. However, the reality is that those already deemed "favorites"—individuals assigned high-profile projects and responsibilities—are effectively pre-selected for advancement. This situation undermines the principle of equal opportunity when exposure to the next level of work is restricted to a select few.

My experience with promotion opportunities reflects these challenges. Despite being a dedicated team member for four years, my interview for promotion was characterized by an unwelcoming and indifferent atmosphere. During the interview, my leadership and people management experience from previous roles were dismissed as irrelevant, and my performance assessments were not accurately communicated to decision-makers. I was accused of missing project deadlines, an untrue and unverified claim. I had consistently met and exceeded project goals ahead of schedule. Although the error was later acknowledged by the project manager and confirmed in writing, the damage to my promotion prospects had already been done, resulting in significant mental stress and self-doubt until the correction was made.

Additionally, during the interview process, there was criticism of the diversity of the interview panel itself. I was informed that my failure to secure the position was due to my responses, but I was also told that other directors on the panel had failed to ask the appropriate questions. This feedback was inconsistent with my previous performance evaluations, consistently highlighting my exceeding expectations. The experience underscored that promotions were not always based on merit or seniority, and the performance evaluation process lacked transparency and alignment with corporate strategy.

The promotion process also revealed a broader issue: Leaders often exhibit territorial behavior, which erodes trust and collaboration across teams and departments. Despite requesting feedback regularly, I found that constructive feedback was hardly provided on time. Then, during performance reviews, feedback was predominantly negative and critical, with little acknowledgment of achievements or strengths. Professional development appeared driven primarily by employee initiative rather than leadership support. Employees were expected to demonstrate their value through new projects and business cases, often without managerial backing.

The absence of equity in decision-making coupled with a lack of managers' understanding of professional development further exacerbates the situation. Training, conferences, and skill-building resources are often inadequate, reflecting a systemic issue where meaningful professional growth and support are not adequately prioritized. It was a daily struggle and a pressure to prove myself. I felt like I am not seen and often dismissed. I had to keep second guessing whether I should speak up or not. It is like walking on eggshells with very little feedback. Some of these struggles are unheard or not experienced by my white counterparts.

Seeking Kinship: I Knew It Couldn't Just Be Me

All the above experiences made me wonder if other minority women felt the same way. I started wondering what it would mean to help women who want to advance in their careers and what roadblocks they face. I started reading the literature and available research on career advancement and promotion opportunities. I realized that trust and managers' confidence in employees are critical to their professional development. I wanted to find the key ingredients necessary in this manager-employee relationship that could help or hinder the promotion process. Is there equity in the promotion process?

This inspired me to do a deep dive into the promotion experiences and realities of minority women in mid-level management who have applied for a promotion five years into their management role. These stories will not only create a shared meaning and belonging for women but also help the managers understand the challenges faced by these women and how they feel supported. Is there a list of behaviors managers exhibit that can help these women with professional growth, self-confidence, and building a relationship of trust? In contrast, can there be behaviors that individuals must pursue to support their advancement? Even further, what can an organization do to help improve opportunities that are considered equitable? The purpose of sharing these stories is for women to learn from each other's experiences and adopt practical tips to navigate the complex corporate labyrinth.

My interview questions were focused on a 360-degree view of the promotion process from the actual posting of the position to promotion decision-making to identify systemic inequities along the way and provide practical tools to reduce biases. While the techniques or strategies for increasing pro-motability I am proposing may sound intuitive, the power lies in the truth and verbiage presented in these techniques. The how in the technique is very clear in the words of the women I interviewed. For example, some narratives include the exact language managers can utilize in their one-on-one meetings, performance evaluations, or professional development discussions. It brings to light the special needs of minority women who are different from others.

An essential step for inspiring change is to understand one's privilege. One person's privilege can be another person's disadvantage and vice versa. Reflecting on one's privilege is the first step to understanding the benefits of the different forms of power in your life and how one can impact those who are disadvantaged. Also, privilege can be contextual because I may feel privileged in one community, setting, and time and underprivileged in a different context and time. It is important to recognize that for yourself.

Growing up in a middle-class family in India, I had the privilege of getting a good education and opportunities. I could explore my creative side by learning five languages. I participated in sports and took vacations with my family to places that not every kid growing up in India could. I could come to the United States to pursue higher studies and support myself. Coming to the US opened a wealth of opportunities for me. To a certain extent, the stereotype of model minority has helped Asians in America succeed and be in the top 90 percent of successful individuals. I also feel privileged to have been brought up with Asian values of a collectivistic approach, respecting everyone, working hard to be successful, striving to be the best, and appreciating different perspectives.

Since an early age, I have been justice oriented and have spoken up anytime I see unjust and unfair treatment toward those around me, my friends, coworkers, family, or myself. I can trust this quality for the greater good of society and be the voice of those who cannot speak for themselves. As a leader,

I would like to lead with humility and principles of servant leadership. It is crucial for leaders to value and recognize the strengths of every member of their team and reward them accordingly. Otherwise, it increases unhealthy competition and the failure of the team to provide desirable results. The article "Respectful Leadership and Followers' Knowledge Sharing: A Social Mindfulness Lens," published in *Human Relations*, coins respectful leadership as other-oriented leadership, where leaders have concern for others on the team and value their perspectives. It is very easy for a leader to be overconfident and blindsided by power.[6] Hence, introspective leaders actively seek feedback, are more self-aware, and are seen as more effective than those who do not.[7] My goal is to emphasize the importance of building a relationship of trust and respect with people you work with as a stepping stone for professional and personal growth and a fulfilling career. I want to call out leaders to engage in self-awareness and self-regulation to recognize their biases and actively seek feedback from their direct reports.

Minority women face unique challenges in corporate America, ranging from systemic bias to a lack of representation in leadership roles. These barriers limit their career growth and hinder the full potential of organizations that fail to leverage diverse talent. To truly understand the depth of these issues, we must first explore the current state of workplace promotions and the entrenched systems that perpetuate these disparities. By examining this foundation, we can identify where change is most urgently needed.

PART I
PROMOTION REALITIES

1
MEET THE WOMEN I INTERVIEWED

IN THIS CHAPTER, I introduce the women whose voices and experiences form the foundation of this book. I chose each participant, using clear inclusion and exclusion criteria to ensure a range of perspectives across industries, roles, and backgrounds. I wanted to highlight women working in diverse environments—from healthcare and human services to corporate and nonprofit spaces. I also explain the questions I asked during our conversations, designed to explore not just their professional journeys but also their internal struggles, moments of doubt, and sources of strength. This chapter sets the stage for the stories that follow, offering insight into who these women are and why their experiences matter.

I interviewed fourteen minority women who held leadership roles in a management capacity or higher working in US-based companies. Eight Fortune 500 companies were represented from five industries: professional services, financial services, retail, airline, healthcare, sales, and information technology. Each woman had at least five years of experience in mid-level management and held a management position in their current company. They represented different ethnicities: eight Asian/Pacific Islanders (from different regions of Southeast Asia), two Hispanic/Latino, and four African American, including two mixed races, identified as African American and Hispanic/Latino. Table 1 describes the women's demographic information, field or work/industry, highest level of education achieved, years of employment, and current job title. The women's names are fictitious but reflect their race/ethnicity while carefully maintaining anonymity and confidentiality. I am hoping that this will create an image of these women in your mind and provide context.

Table 1

Women's Demographics, Industry, Highest Education, Years of Experience, and Job Title

	Race/Ethnicity	Field/Industry	Highest Education	Years Employed	Title
Tara	Asian/Pacific Islander	Airline	Bachelor's	7	IT Product Owner
Renell	Hispanic/ Latino Multi-Racial	Technology	Bachelor's	0.5	Director
Sheniqua	African American	Non-Profit Social Work	Master's	1	Community Organizer
Cynthia	Hispanic/ Latino	Non-Profit Human Services	Master's	10	Senior Director
Rita	Asian/Pacific Islander	Financial Services	Bachelor's	3	Senior Director
Serena	African American Multi-Racial	Technology/ Sales	Bachelor's	7	Head of Industry

	Race/Ethnicity	Field/Industry	Highest Education	Years Employed	Title
Diva	Asian/Pacific Islander	Healthcare/ Pharmaceutical	Master's	10	Program Manager
Sima	Asian/Pacific Islander	Technology	Master's	12	Manager
Jaya	Asian/Pacific Islander	Non-Profit/ Technology	Master's	25	Director
Chanell	African American	Management Consulting	Master's	2	Lead-Data Analytics
Sue	Asian/Pacific Islander	Consulting Office/Business Operations	Bachelor's	6	Manager
Maya	Asian/Pacific Islander	Human Resources/ Learning and Development	Master's	6	Director
Jing	Asian/Pacific Islander	Non-Profit Health Care	Doctorate	16	Project Director
Naomi	African American	Luxury Retail Management	Bachelor's	4	Team Manager

I chose to focus on women in mid-level management because the underrepresentation of women in senior leadership makes this a critical stage where many of their struggles, doubts, and aspirations are most visible — before they break through to the top.

These are women who have been in management for around five years — a point in their careers that, in my view, often marks a readiness for the next big step. It's a stage where experience meets ambition, and where questions about leadership potential and promotion become especially pressing. All these women have either applied for a promotion and been passed up or have successfully received one, offering a rich and nuanced view of what this transition truly looks like.

Collectively, these women identified themselves as female and Black, Latina, Asian, American Indian or Alaskan Native,

Native Hawaiian, Pacific Islander, or mixed-race women. According to the Fair Labor Standards Act, a salaried employee is a worker who is paid a set amount of money or compensation, otherwise known as salary, on a consistent pay basis. The women identified their employment status (as full-time) through their pay stubs provided by the company. Mid-level managers included women who were managers, senior managers, associate directors, directors, or equivalent titles, with or without direct reports. A promotion was defined as a change in grade level and/or title along with a commensurate increase in responsibility and pay.[8]

I intentionally excluded occupations that are heavily dominated by either men—such as construction, maintenance, transportation, military, and law enforcement—or by women—such as education, social services, personal care, and direct patient care. I made this choice to avoid occupational biases or gender-based stereotypes that could influence the findings. My goal was to focus on women working in fields where gender representation is more balanced, allowing for a clearer look at their experiences with advancement. Additionally, I did not count lateral moves within an organization—those that didn't involve a change in grade level or rank—as promotions for the purposes of my work.

When I began this project, I wanted to understand something that had long gone unspoken in many workplaces: What does it really feel like to be a minority woman trying to get promoted? I was curious about more than just statistics or policies; I wanted to hear real stories, from real women, navigating the complex terrain of ambition, recognition, and leadership.

So, I asked: What are the experiences of minority women as they seek promotion within their organizations? Do they believe the process is fair and equitable? What specific moments, patterns, or dynamics shape that perception? And perhaps most importantly, how does the relationship between a woman and her manager—the person often making or influencing the promotion decision—affect the outcome?

These conversations went far beyond checklists and resumes; they opened a window into how these women interpreted the decisions made about them, how they experienced encouragement or dismissal, and how they carried both self-doubt and determination.

These interviews were rich with insight and honesty. Throughout this book, I've woven their voices into the narrative to show not just what they've experienced but how they've made sense of it—and what that reveals about the workplace systems we take for granted.

The statistics and stories reveal a troubling pattern of inequity in promotions for minority women, but they also highlight areas where progress is possible. Efforts to address these disparities often fall under the umbrella of diversity, equity, and inclusion (DEI) initiatives. Strong evidence links DEI activities to employee satisfaction, productivity, and overall business performance. However, these programs vary widely in their effectiveness. Understanding the current landscape of DEI efforts—what's working, what's not, and why—provides critical insights into how we can build more equitable workplaces.

2
REVISIONING DEI

Shift of Power: Collective Leadership

THE DISCUSSION OF equity is incomplete without understanding the reciprocal relationship between power, privilege, and discrimination. With power comes a sense of privilege and authority to make decisions for those who do not have power. Abuse of power can lead to discrimination and unjust treatment, and the vicious cycle continues. Leaders are in a position of power to make decisions for followers. They can use this power to create a cohesive team where every member feels safe to make autonomous decisions and exercise their leadership skills for collective growth, also called Laissez-Faire leadership. It gets challenging when leaders and managers expect the employees to follow the same decision-making patterns and take the same approach to problem-solving as they would while compromising the individuality or uniqueness of every employee. Leaders deliberately withhold or restrict information to maintain control, power, and influence. This practice can negatively impact organizational effectiveness and culture, impede collaboration, and lead to frustration and resistance to change.

If leaders focus on the end goal and the employees' intentions and allow them to execute the tasks utilizing their unique skills while guiding and providing support and feedback when needed, the outcome will be the same, and the satisfaction will be multifold. Just as a mango tree bends down when the fruit ripens for us to enjoy, power must bring humility for its true benefit. There is power in providing freedom and allowing others to make their own choices. There is power in respecting others and accepting different viewpoints. There is power in collective leadership and shared values rather than dictating to others or adopting an autocratic leadership style. Power sharing ensures that decisions are made with input from a diverse range of stakeholders rather than being concentrated in the hands of a few. Employees feel empowered to contribute ideas, take on leadership roles, and participate in key decisions.

Collective leadership allows each team member to be accountable for the team's performance.[9] Companies with a lateral rather than a hierarchical structure allow for the building of the leadership capacity and knowledge of the team. Spreading out leadership responsibilities and authority can help develop future leaders, foster a collaborative work culture, and reduce the risk of burnout among top executives. Last, transparent communication channels allow for the free exchange of information, which helps build trust and cooperation within the organization.

Pay, Promotions, and Rewards

It is well established that women, particularly minority women, are underrepresented in C-suite and executive positions and are underpaid. Based on Women in the Labor Force: a Databook (2024) by the Bureau of Labor Statistics, the median weekly earnings of women chief executives ($2,277) is 78.3 percent of men chief executives ($2,908) in management and related professions per 2022 annual averages.[10] Men in corporate sectors typically assume high-status and high-paying jobs that require allocating resources and client engagement. In contrast, women assume internal low-paying roles that do not require strategic decision-making.[11] Women and minorities often do not get an opportunity to do the glamorous work that white men do, and many face a systemic barrier that prevents them from breaking through the "glass ceiling."

The number of minority women who do not seek promotion to senior leadership positions until retirement age is proportionately higher than any other gender or ethnicity represented in the Federal Government despite higher education, prominent leadership potential, and strong position capability.[12] Studies of women working in male-dominated careers, such as technical fields, military, and law enforcement, indicate that they opt out of promotions for personal reasons, including childcare, unwillingness to compromise on personal commitments, cultural reasons, and sexism in leadership roles at the organizational level.[13] Furthermore, White women, but not minority women, experience something akin to a "glass escalator," whereby they are promoted into management only in marginal increments and rarely to the highest positions of power. However, those promotions are a smaller step up—more of a step stool than an escalator.[14] Such inequities in promotions and pay indicate an underlying discrimination.

Discrimination in promotion processes occurs while allocating promotions and making salary determinations. There are three types of discrimination:[15]

1. Allocative discrimination is when women and minorities are sought for specific kinds of jobs with specific pay through promotion.

   For example, consider Nina, a talented project manager at a company who consistently delivers excellent results. When a senior leadership role opens in a high-profile department, Nina notices she is being encouraged to apply instead for a less influential position typically filled by women or minority employees. Meanwhile, her white male colleague Jake is fast-tracked for the top leadership role with higher pay. This steering of women and minorities toward roles with limited advancement or lower pay demonstrates allocative discrimination.

2. Within-job wage disparity is when women and minorities receive lower salaries than white male counterparts within a given occupation.

   For instance, Carlos and Jake both hold the same position as senior data analysts, with similar qualifications and performance records. However, Carlos discovers that Jake earns significantly more, despite doing the same work. This difference in pay for the same job reflects within-job wage disparity.

3. Valuative discrimination occurs when women and minorities with equal skills in female- and minority-dominated occupations are paid lower salaries because they are valued less.

   As an example, Asha is a licensed clinical social worker, a role requiring advanced education and critical skills. Despite comparable qualifications and workload, she earns much less than Tom, a network administrator in a male-dominated tech field. The lower pay for Asha's work reflects valuative discrimination, where occupations dominated by women or minorities are undervalued financially, regardless of skill or responsibility.

Such disparities have spurred some organizations to make systemic changes to make hiring, promotion, and compensation practices more equitable. Events such as hate crimes against the Asian American Pacific Islander (AA/PI) community, the death of George Floyd, the immigration crisis at the United States border, and violence against African Americans have created a sense of urgency for companies to pay special attention to diversity, equity, and inclusion (DEI). Although most studies have viewed race as a constraint that must be managed (e.g., bias against perceived marginality), some researchers present race as a resource through which negative experiences can be turned into constructive change and collective meaning.[16]

Increasingly, professional groups of minority women are emerging that allow for mentorship and programs that inspire and uplift professional minority women across the country, such as The National Association of Asian American Professionals, The National Black MBA Association, The National Organization for Women, The National Society of Hispanic Professionals, CHIEF, Lean IN, etc. As a result, women and racial or ethnic minorities are better equipped to navigate the White boys club and pave their way to higher ranks of leadership. Membership in such groups gives women a sense of psychological safety and validation of their struggles. The most significant benefit of participation in such groups is mentorship, which is vital for career advancement.

Another obstacle to fairness in promotion is the reluctance to promote from within. It is typical for organizations to hire talent, specifically for C-Suite roles, from outside the organization rather than considering capable employees for promotion from within their teams or the organization. According to the 2019 Deloitte Global Human Capital Trends Report,[17]

> Rather than searching to find and hire great leaders from the outside who may or may not succeed in the organization's corporate culture, most organizations would do well to explore new approaches and invest more in developing the potential leaders they have. (p. 41)

This is validated for sales and marketing positions that support the efficacy of hiring at entry-level positions in sales and promoting from within, as evidenced by increased salespersons' trust in the organization and reduced staff turnover. Moreover, Internal employees have transaction-specific skills about the companies' policies, products, and customers. It also costs companies more to hire from outside the organization, and training for these respective positions takes longer.[18]

Although there is a clear incentive to promote internal employees, minority employees with long tenure with the necessary skills, knowledge, and qualifications are not considered for promotion and succession planning, resulting in a high turnover of diverse talent. According to the Women in the Workplace 2021 report by McKinsey & Company,[19] which surveyed a quarter of a million people on their work experience across 750 companies between 2015 and 2021, minority women dropped off by more than 75 percent at every step of the promotion pipeline between entry-level and C-suite positions This resulted in only 4 percent of minority women in C-suite positions. Their most recent report further supported this trend with the following findings:[20] "For every 100 men who are promoted from entry-level roles to manager positions, only 87 women are promoted, and only 82 women of color are promoted. Only one in four C-Suite leaders is a woman, and only one in 20 is a woman of color."

Survey data was collected from employees in three organizations: a city government (N = 369), a law enforcement agency (N = 653), and the US military (N = 15,497).[21] They used these data to study selective incivility related to turnover intentions and found that the more people face rudeness on the job, the more they consider leaving. Their findings support the likelihood that uncivil treatment drives some women and people of color out of their places of work. The stories of minority women in this book highlight real examples of many such forms of discrimination and validate existing research on barriers faced by women seeking promotions and reasons for dropping out of the race.

Impact of COVID-19

According to the Women in the Workplace 2021 report by McKinsey & Company,[19] the pandemic continued to further challenges for women by escalating the burnout typically experienced by women in the workplace. They found that one in four women considered downshifting their career or leaving the workforce a few months into the pandemic—a higher percentage than their male counterparts. In 2021, 42 percent of women said they had been often or almost always burned out compared to 32 percent a year ago, especially women experiencing a disability. Women with disabilities were about twice as likely to say that requesting a flexible work schedule, taking time off for mental health reasons, and setting boundaries around availability had hurt their careers. Furthermore, during the pandemic, as the economies experienced significant changes, women's earnings declined from 2020 to 2022, causing a financial burden due to high inflation.

One major cause of burnout during the pandemic was having to care for children and older adults, such as elderly family members, at the same time. Such "double duty" caregivers were more than likely women who experienced burnout and/or considered downshifting their careers or leaving the workforce entirely. As per the United States Bureau of Labor Statistics 2022, in 2021, women comprised 56.1 percent of the labor force, down 1.3 percent from 2019 before COVID-19. Men's labor force participation (although it also plummeted to 1.6 percent lower from 2019) remained much higher (at 67.6 percent) than women's. Moreover, women accounted for 52 percent of all workers in management, professional, and related occupations, more than their share of total employment (47 percent in management, professional, and related occupations).[22] Intersectionality of race, ethnicity, and gender created more challenges for women during the pandemic. One in four Asian women, particularly East Asian women, were impacted by anti-Asian hate due to the COVID-19 pandemic. They were more likely to experience microaggressions, felt that promotions were not based on objective criteria, and expressed unhappiness with their company.[19] The complications of COVID-19 thus exacerbated existing problems around promotion.

Occupational Stereotypes and Perceptions

When comparing earnings by race and ethnicity, earnings differences between women and men were largest among Asians and Whites. Asian women earned 79 percent as much as Asian men and White women earned 83 percent as much as White men. The impact of individual and cultural factors of individuals working in male- and female-dominated occupations (N = 144) on gender, race, and prestige of various occupations was studied.[23] The results indicated that male-dominated occupations, or those performed by White people, were perceived as higher in status than those performed by Black people or both races equally.

Occupational stereotyping continues to exist in the United States in part due to perceptions of individuals who pursue gender-atypical fields. For example, women in male-dominated fields are typically praised for being progressive. In contrast, men in female-dominated fields are criticized for settling for lower pay and less status than men in male-dominated fields. Moreover, men in female-dominated fields are perceived as less masculine than men who work in masculine fields. Although women are increasingly being accepted in male-dominated careers, women tend to pursue gender-typical fields because of lower self-concept, a tendency to be viewed as more masculine than women in typically feminine occupational roles, and fear of failure.

In addition to gender, race also plays a significant role in occupational stereotyping. A study conducted with White male and female mid-level managers aged twenty-four to sixty-three associated White managers with traits of being successful managers more than African American managers. The decision-makers interviewing African American candidates blamed poor job performance on negative stereotypes they had regarding Blacks for not selecting them for promotions.[24] This results in hesitation among minorities to consider entering predominantly White occupational settings.

These gaps raised important questions that couldn't be answered by policies or data alone—which is why I turned to the voices of women themselves. I wanted to understand what career development truly looks like within their organizations, and how their lived experiences reflect or challenge the structures around them.

Career Advancement Opportunities

When I spoke with women about career advancement opportunities within their companies, they attested that there has been a turning point since the death of George Floyd. (See Table 1 for details.) Women reported that companies have shifted their focus to embracing DEI efforts, especially Fortune 500 companies, which had an infrastructure for diversity and inclusion but were not actively pursuing it. DEI is now at the forefront of hiring, promotion, and retention practices.

An Asian woman, Sue, an office manager overseeing business operations for six years in a large technology consulting firm in the Midwest, said, "We now have regular access to DEI metrics." It continues to be aspirational and not as intuitive or intentional for some companies. On the contrary, Rita, a Southeast Asian woman working as a senior director in financial services at a life insurance company (ranked 110th in Fortune 500 companies in 2024) with predominantly white men in the C-Suite, expressed concerns about the inclusion and focus on diversity for the promotion decision-making. She stated, "When we are very worried about the lack of women in senior leadership positions at a company, our number one candidate happens to be a woman who is a minority, and we miss this obvious opportunity, we have to find a way to fix this."

While most women shared that their companies are forthcoming in supporting career growth and provide equal advancement opportunities for everyone, Serena, who was a head of industry with a large renowned technology giant in technology sales, said, "It takes an average amount of years between each level to get to the next level, and the higher you climb in a level, the longer it takes in between." Another roadblock reported by the women is when each job is associated with a level band and employees' salary cap is at that level, they feel stuck. Individuals must find a new role in a level band in which they can get promoted, and fewer people move out of those roles, or the positions do not become available easily. This makes it more difficult to get promotion opportunities. She reported that retaining top performers disincentivizes others who are waiting in queue for promotion. Chanell, a Black woman who worked as a lead in data analytics in a US-based business and technology consulting firm with around 2,000 employees, validated this. She felt that new ideas are unwelcome or funded when a company has long-tenured employees with similar mindsets. Chanell quoted, "More innovative ideas that are more strategic in nature don't tend to come to life as fast as I'd like them to, or I feel that I have to do advocacy for them to understand."

Career Advancement Programs

This section includes a summary of the women's responses to the question, "What is your company's philosophy on career advancement and professional growth of employees? What does it look like in practice for individuals with diverse backgrounds and cultures?" Table 2 shows the distribution of different career advancement programs.

Table 2

Distribution of Career Advancement Programs

Career Advancement Programs	Number of Women Recommended
Training and Professional Development	7
Individual Career Development Plan	7
Employee Resource Groups	3
Mentorship	5
Recognition and Rewards	1

❯ Training and Professional Development

Seven women referenced skill-building courses and professional development classes as beneficial for career advancement. These include topics on how to be a leader, lead a meeting, improve presentation skills, crucial conversations, Six Sigma Greenbelt training, managerial skills, and so on. Such professional development opportunities are available through LinkedIn learning, online communities, and in-person courses. Different types of training are available to employees based on their grade level, and training is allotted based on a specific career development plan.

Women found these trainings, seminars, or classes valuable and say they create an opportunity for underrepresented groups to practice, gain confidence, and be prepared for promotion opportunities. They also provide an outlet for experts to teach and refine their skills. Naomi, an African American team manager who worked in an international luxury fashion company in retail management, was nominated for an eighteen-month professional development program geared toward promotion to the next level. Naomi reported that her manager was also in a senior leadership program, which is more global and would prepare her for the role of vice president.

Maya, a human resources learning and development director of a talent development team with 18,000 employees, said their learning management system has over 8,000 courses of different types of learning, including communication skills, technical skills, technical tools, active listening, empathy skills, and so on. The learning management system allows employees to learn, practice, and apply professional skills to develop themselves.

Tara worked for a top international airline industry as a product owner and was also selected for a professional development and leadership program. She said, "Asian and minority women are cherry-picked because they fit the demographics to be part of this program that would develop us into the next level management positions."

▶ Individual Career Development Plan

Seven women reported that their company provides a path to growth and room for promotion. Shaniqua, a Black woman working for a Black family-owned business, reported that the company executive director was willing to create positions and titles and provide raises to employees who stated there was no room for promotion because the company would likely promote from within their family.

Rita stated that promoting from within and collaborating with various departments about promotion opportunities is part of their company culture. Diva, a Southeast Asian program manager, represented a big pharmaceutical company wherein each division has an HR generalist with whom employees work to develop a career development plan. Employees then have a conversation with their manager to develop specific goals with timeframes to advance to a senior level. This company also recently reviewed and consolidated all positions and job titles to provide clear guidelines to managers.

Chanell mentioned career advisors do performance evaluations and are present for calibration meetings to help employees with their career goals. She explained, "They do a pretty good job of saying what exactly you must do to get to the next level. We have career advisors who may or may not be part of our project who do exactly that."

Maya mentioned that her company has a skills-based career growth model for each business function, which is included in a guide that employees can reference to guide discussions with their managers about how they want to grow in their careers. The company has a quarterly continuous performance review process with active professional development conversations about job shadowing, stretch opportunities, and more.

▶ Employee Resource Groups (ERGs)

Affinity groups, also known as employee resource groups (ERGs) are networks of employees that form based on shared characteristics or background, sponsored by the organization they work for. It brings together employees with similar backgrounds or interests and can have a powerful influence in the workplace.

Three women represented companies that have employee resource groups, such as the Asian group that celebrates holidays like the Lunar New Year. Although these groups have received more marketing and support in the last three or four years, they existed before. As per Sue, ERGs collaborate with other groups and talent development teams to ensure speaking up and coaching sessions to support minority or underrepresented groups to find their footing and fulfillment in the corporate world. She also mentioned specific programs that allow people to bring their passion to workplace social communities, which can also include a cultural element and are different from ERGs. Sue shared about women's leadership networks, which are not limited to women.

Men and other allies are invited for inclusivity because their involvement invites diverse messaging. For example, it was relayed that women present during meetings/sessions often tend to upspeak or display body language that exhibits nervousness or a lack of confidence. Such groups allow for discussions on tips and strategies to deal with someone who, for example, may respond condescendingly while the individual is trying to present or speak up. It also allowed the men in these sessions to see what it is like for a woman to present or speak up in a group setting.

Maya reported that colleagues who led ERGs, such as the Asian Pacific group, women's professional group, virtual professionals' network, young professionals' network, Veterans group, etc., do other activities that can provide and foster professional development.

▶ Mentorship

Five women with whom I talked shared about mentorship programs within their companies that focus on minorities or underrepresented groups.

Serena reported leading a Black community group in an elite sales organization and starting this program so mentees could learn from mentors who look like them. Leaders unconsciously mentor people like them in a homogenous majority leadership, and the homogeneity grows. There are similar underrepresented groups in the US sector, such as Black, Native, and Latinx groups, and other groups more globally for women that are geared toward leadership roles.

Sima, a manager of Southeast Asian descent working for a worldwide leader in technology solutions, mentioned that there are mentorship programs employees can apply for based on their performance and conversations with their managers. Once you are selected, there are different buckets or areas where you can grow, such as technical or finance. They then have a committee responsible for assigning the right mentor based on an individual's goals and interests for the next three years.

Jing, an Asian woman who worked in a global healthcare company, reported receiving mentorship from a minority senior leader with whom she was working on a high-visibility project. While the company does not offer mentorship officially, she was a recipient of this because of her proximity to this senior leader. She reported feeling confident and trusted to represent the company with important stakeholders because of this intentional mentorship and exposure to higher-level discussions.

▶ Recognition and Rewards

Maya reported that her organization has a recognition program for colleagues to recognize each other. This may result in a monetary reward, a promotion, or a role change. She was offered a higher title for social media and company communications, more vacation, and stock options as a reward before a promotion, for which she received the official title and salary raise.

While career development programs provide essential support for minority professionals, their long-term impact depends on how deeply DEI principles are embedded in an organization's culture and strategy. To move beyond surface-level interventions, we must confront the shifting realities of diversity, equity, and inclusion in today's social and political climate.

The next section redefines what DEI means in this moment—moving past performative gestures to a framework rooted in accountability, measurable value, and resilience in the face of backlash. It offers a business case for why DEI still matters and outlines tangible steps organizations can take to move forward with clarity, courage, and sustained commitment.

FROM CONCEPT TO MEANINGFUL ACTION

The DEI Dilemma: Navigating the Whiplash

Several major corporations, previously perceived as champions of diversity, equity, and inclusion (DEI), have made headlines for disbanding their DEI teams in 2024. This shift has sparked significant debate about the authenticity and long-term commitment to DEI practices within these organizations. For instance, Microsoft's recent decision to lay off its DEI leader has been particularly notable, as reported by Business Insider.[25] This move has drawn criticism and raised questions about the sincerity of the company's previous DEI efforts.

The departure of DEI teams from prominent corporations, which often did not demonstrate a deep ideological commitment to these principles but engaged in performative actions, sends a troubling message. While some international and global companies have successfully integrated DEI into their operations due to their diverse leadership and regional representation, the layoffs signal a retreat from these values. This retreat can adversely affect perceptions among smaller companies and those with predominantly homogeneous workforces. These companies might now use the actions of larger tech giants as a justification for their lack of DEI initiatives, reinforcing a culture of exclusion rather than fostering genuine inclusivity.

The implications of these layoffs extend beyond individual companies and highlight a broader issue within the corporate world. The dismantling of DEI teams in organizations that previously emphasized their importance can perpetuate a culture of tokenism and undermine the progress made in diversifying corporate environments. For smaller enterprises and those still evolving their DEI strategies, this development may serve as a misguided excuse to delay or forego meaningful DEI implementation, potentially stalling critical efforts to build more inclusive workplaces. This can result in decreased morale, reduced engagement, and potentially increased turnover among marginalized groups. As the corporate landscape grapples with these challenges, it becomes increasingly crucial for organizations to reaffirm their commitment to DEI, ensuring these principles are deeply embedded in their culture rather than treated as transient trends.

Redefining DEI: A Shift in Focus

The current discourse around the whiplash effect in DEI strategies primarily focuses on the abrupt and often contradictory shifts in corporate commitment to DEI initiatives. As large corporations reassess or dismantle their DEI teams, the broader implications for organizational culture and employee morale are coming under scrutiny.

There is a need to focus on people for who they are, their unique contributions, and their unique selves. While promoting equity and inclusion, it is equally important to be mindful of the potential for reverse discrimination. Fairness must extend to all individuals, ensuring that no one feels overlooked or undervalued due to efforts to correct historic imbalances. The goal is to create a culture where each person is valued for their unique skills, experiences, and contributions—regardless of background—so that opportunity is truly inclusive and merit-based.

Regardless of what we call this initiative, there is clear evidence showing the positive impact of focusing on employee engagement and experience on employee satisfaction, productivity, and innovation, ultimately enhancing business performance and growth. Hence, there is a need to rebrand DEI for true value and call it the Department of People Experience (DPE), whose focus would be on all people and hiring for the unique experiences all people bring to the workforce.

Business Case: Real Impact

1. Enhances Employee Satisfaction and Engagement

   - Increased Retention and Reduced Turnover: A McKinsey & Company (2020) study[26] found that organizations in the top quartile for diversity experience higher employee satisfaction and are 35 percent more likely to outperform their less diverse peers. When people see themselves reflected in their workplace, they're more likely to stay—and more likely to help the business succeed.

   - Sense of Belonging: When people feel like they truly belong at work, everything changes. According to a 2021 study by BetterUp[27], that sense of belonging boosts job performance by 56 percent, cuts the risk of quitting in half, and leads to 75 percent fewer sick days. When you feel connected, you show up stronger, stay longer, and feel better doing it.

   - Psychological Safety and Innovation: Research from *Harvard Business Review* (2017)[28] shows that when the workplace feels truly inclusive, people show up differently. Employees are 3.5 times more likely to bring their full potential, leading to higher engagement, greater satisfaction, and stronger results across the board.

2. Drives Productivity and Innovation

   - Higher Team Performance: A 2018 study by Boston Consulting Group[29] found that companies with diverse leadership teams see nearly 20 percent more revenue from innovation. When different voices are at the table, fresh ideas turn into real results.

- Cognitive Diversity Leads to Better Problem Solving: A 2014 study published in Proceedings of the National Academy of Sciences[30] found that teams with a mix of backgrounds and perspectives are better at solving tough problems than teams that all think alike. Different minds approach challenges in different ways—and that leads to better solutions.

- Inclusive Workplaces Reduce Absenteeism: The Center for American Progress reported in 2012[31] that when people don't feel included at work—or worse, face discrimination—it costs businesses big. In fact, turnover and absenteeism tied to those issues add up to $64 billion a year in lost productivity.

3. Positively Impacts Financial Performance

- Higher Profitability: A 2020 McKinsey & Company[26] report found that companies with more women on their executive teams were 25 percent more likely to outperform their peers in profits. When those teams also reflected ethnic diversity, the odds jumped to 36 percent. Bottom line: The more diverse the leadership, the stronger the results.

- Increased Market Share: Deloitte's 2018[32] research found that companies with inclusive cultures don't just feel better; they perform better. These organizations are twice as likely to hit their financial goals and six times more likely to be innovative and adaptable. Inclusion fuels progress on every level.

4. Legal and Compliance Benefits

- Mitigating Risk: Programs that promote inclusion and fairness improve culture and protect the bottom line. According to the EEOC (2021)[33], avoiding issues like discrimination and harassment can save companies millions in legal costs and settlements.

- Attracting Top Talent: A 2020 Glassdoor[34] survey found that most job seekers—76 percent—care about workplace diversity when deciding where to work. For many, it's not just a bonus; it's a deciding factor.

Reevaluate the Need for DEI Programs: Making an Informed Decision

I recommend that organizations take a comprehensive and intentional approach when evaluating the need for DEI programs.

Organizations can evaluate the need for DEI programs through several key approaches:

1. Assessing Organizational Impact: Evaluate the current state of DEI within the organization by conducting surveys and gathering employee feedback. Understanding the gaps in diversity, equity, and inclusion can help determine the specific needs and areas for improvement.

2. Analyzing Business Outcomes: Review how DEI initiatives impact business performance metrics, such as employee retention, innovation, and customer satisfaction. Analyzing these metrics can provide insights into the effectiveness and value of DEI programs.

3. Benchmarking Against Industry Standards: Compare the organization's DEI practices with industry standards and best practices. This benchmarking can help identify areas where the organization is falling short and improvements can be made.

4. Engaging Leadership and Stakeholders: Ensure senior leadership and key stakeholders are involved in the evaluation process. Their commitment and support are crucial for the success of DEI initiatives and for integrating DEI into the broader organizational strategy.

5. Setting Clear Objectives and Metrics: Establish clear objectives and metrics for DEI programs. This includes setting measurable goals for diversity representation, career advancement equity, and workplace culture inclusion. Regularly review and adjust these metrics to align with the organization's evolving needs.

6. Fostering Continuous Improvement: Recognize that DEI is an ongoing journey rather than a one-time initiative. Continuously assess the effectiveness of DEI programs and be prepared to adjust based on feedback and changing organizational dynamics.

In summary, the current whiplash in DEI efforts reflects deeper issues regarding corporations' authenticity and long-term commitment to these values. To effectively evaluate the need for DEI programs, organizations must assess their impact, compare them against industry benchmarks, engage stakeholders, and focus on continuous improvement.

Regardless of a company's current DEI strategy or the presence of a dedicated DEI office, ensuring fairness in the allocation of promotions and rewards remains a critical concern for organizations. My goal is to focus on advancing this equity by offering targeted strategies for HR professionals, employees, and managers. These strategies aim to ensure that promotion decisions, rewards, and opportunities for professional development are handled equitably, fostering a fair and transparent environment for career growth and advancement.

Hence, I believe that investing in all people and their experiences is not just a moral imperative but a strategic business advantage. Companies with a strong focus on all persons for their unique backgrounds and creativity ensure higher employee satisfaction, increased productivity, stronger financial performance, and reduced legal risks. As workforce expectations shift, organizations that fail to encourage employees to bring their authentic selves to work risk falling behind competitors that leverage diversity for innovation and growth.

Despite legislative efforts to demote diversity, equity, and inclusion, many minority women still find themselves fighting for the same recognition and opportunities as their peers. While DEI initiatives aim to create fairness, their real-world impact often falls short. Equity and fairness are not just moral imperatives; they directly influence employee satisfaction, retention, and overall workplace culture. At the same time, concerns about reverse discrimination highlight the need for solutions that benefit everyone, regardless of race, gender, or background. Actual progress means ensuring that no one is left behind or unfairly advantaged. To understand where these efforts succeed—and where they fail—we must examine women's daily realities in corporate America and explore strategies that create lasting, meaningful change for all.

3
THRIVING OR SURVIVING

MINORITY WOMEN OFTEN find themselves at opposite ends of the spectrum in the workplace, experiencing either significant struggles or notable success. On one end, many minority women face substantial barriers when it comes to promotions and rewards. They frequently encounter challenges in gaining visibility, recognition, and opportunities for advancement, particularly for high-level executive roles. These obstacles can stem from systemic biases, lack of representation, and the often-unconscious prejudices that skew perceptions of competence and leadership potential. Consequently, minority women may struggle to be seen and heard, finding it difficult to receive the same level of acknowledgment and support that may come more naturally to their white counterparts.

Conversely, at the other end of the continuum, some minority women thrive in their careers, thanks to the support of senior leadership and managers who can look beyond surface-level characteristics and recognize the value of diverse perspectives. In such environments, these leaders appreciate the unique contributions that minority women bring, such as divergent thinking and creative problem-solving abilities. This recognition and support can significantly enhance career prospects and professional development, enabling minority women to achieve success and visibility that might otherwise be elusive.

The disparity between these two experiences underscores a critical issue in workplace equity. While some minority women benefit from inclusive leadership that values diversity, many others face ongoing challenges to achieve the same recognition and opportunities. The contrast highlights a broader systemic issue, where the basic accolades and project opportunities that may be more readily accessible to white women require a far greater struggle for minority women. Addressing these disparities involves a concerted effort to ensure that all employees, regardless of their background, have equal access to career advancement and are fairly recognized for their contributions.

Women and members of minorities experience a glass ceiling or barriers to advancement in the workplace and receive lower rewards, such as pay, promotion, and training opportunities.[3] In the 1980s and 1990s, women were promoted to less critical positions, such as public relations or roles that require technical expertise rather than decision-making responsibilities to create the appearance of increasing opportunities.[7] During those times, job conditions were unfavorable to career success. This had to do with perceptual distortions associated with the "token status" of female and minority managers in work groups rather than demographic attributes alone.[35]

While the glass ceiling prevents women and underrepresented minority groups from attaining leadership positions, the glass cliff is a condition in which minorities are more likely to receive promotion into leadership positions, but only in underperforming organizations or in roles that are difficult and carry significant risk.[36] This predisposes these individuals to criticism, failure, and blame for adverse outcomes.

Minority women are CEOs in Fortune 500 companies at a higher rate than non-Fortune 500 companies.[37] Additionally, gender matching is another phenomenon that causes bias in senior-level promotions, whereby executive openings are filled with the incumbent's gender. Given that women and minorities have token representation in Fortune 500 companies, the matching concept further delays change.[38]

In 2021, women comprised 56.1 percent of the labor force, down 1.3 percent from 2019 before COVID-19. Men's labor force participation (although it also plummeted to 1.6 percent lower from 2019) remained much higher (at 67.6 percent) than women's.[22] Moreover, women accounted for 52 percent of all workers in management, professional, and related occupations, more than their share of total employment (47 percent in management, professional, and related occupations).

The research on gender differences in promotability indicates that women who meet the social role expectations of their managers, receive positive evaluations, and are liked by their managers have higher chances of career advancement. Men consider aggressive and direct behavior atypical of women. Assertiveness is interpreted as unfriendly, which can lead to backlash or negative reactions.[39]

How do women overcome their social role barriers or prevent backlash from violating gender role expectations in the workplace? "Political skill is an indispensable tool for female executives to achieve their career objectives."[39] A study done in 2018 measured the outcome of voice (or speaking-up behavior) by articulating how it impacts the social status of men and women and whether they are considered leaders. This research included a three-way field study and an experiment that found that "men who spoke up promotively benefited the most in terms of status and leader emergence, not only compared to men who spoke up prohibitively but also to women who spoke up promotively."[40]

Women in the workforce often experience more than one reality or identity, resulting in multiple challenges due to the intersection of race, gender, sexual orientation, religious affiliation, power differential, in-group/out-group dynamics, etc. "Intersectionality is not this grand theory that covers all the unjust practices for everyone. It is the intersection of unjust practices that happen to specific individuals or sub-groups of people at a given point in time."[41]

According to a McKinsey & Company 2021 report[19], lesbian and bisexual women do not feel comfortable bringing their whole selves to work because they often receive negative feedback, such as they are too outspoken and confrontational. Almost half of all lesbian and bisexual women feel as though they must be careful when talking about their personal lives in their workplace. They are also significantly more likely than women with other gender identities to feel uncomfortable sharing their work-life challenges and to experience burnout with colleagues.

This report also identified that compared to women of other races and ethnicities, Latinas are less likely to say they have the flexibility to take time off for family or personal reasons. They are also less likely to leave work to deal with unexpected events. These numbers are even lower for Latinas who are immigrants. Currently, 43 percent of Latinas spend five or more hours daily on housework and caregiving, compared to only 34 percent of women overall.

Based on the findings of this report, Black women are facing disproportionately high barriers in the workplace. Black women experience bias in hiring and promotions. They receive promotions at a lower rate than White women at the first step up to manager, and more than a quarter of Black women say their race has led them to miss an opportunity to advance. They experience more microaggressions than other groups of women and are three to four times more likely than White women to be subject to disrespectful and "othering" comments and behavior. To add to their burden, Black women are far more likely than other employees to be coping with the impact of racism and racial trauma.

According to the 2022 report by McKinsey & Company[20], Black and Latina women are less likely than women of other races and ethnicities to report that their manager supports their career development. Latina and Black women experience less psychological safety. Less than half reported that their team members are not penalized for their mistakes. These barriers, microaggressions, and stereotypes further perpetuate the glass ceiling. My attempt is to explore such unique circumstances and challenges experienced by minority women in their own words and to understand how these interplay in decision-making for promotions.

After exploring these structural and interpersonal barriers, I chose to gather women's thoughts and perceptions on workplace discrimination to better understand how these dynamics show up in their daily experiences—and how they impact their career trajectories, confidence, and sense of belonging.

Perceptions of Minority Women in Mid-Level Management

The information obtained from interviews validate the literature regarding the lack of representation of minority women in senior leadership or executive positions. All but four women reported that C-suite leaders were all White and predominantly male. Two of four women who reported favoring diverse representation in senior leadership roles reported that their company could do better to increase representation within different diverse subgroups, especially at mid-level management. Sheniqua worked for an all-Black, family-owned business, and the culture in this company was to promote professional development. However, Black male owners did not welcome the ideas of Black women managers and neither trusted their leadership abilities. Diva, who worked for a large technology company, reported that White men and Asian American Pacific Islander men were not considered a minority in their field as C-suite positions in this industry are primarily populated by them. Hence, they focus career growth promotion efforts on Hispanic/Latino and Native/Alaskan Indian employees. Rita said, "We have diversity, equity, and inclusion (DEI) as a big part of our HR goals, but I don't know we have arrived where we want to be in practice. As you get more senior in the insurance industry, the workforce is increasingly White and male."

Table 3

Sentiment Analysis of Being a Minority Woman in Mid-Level Management

Participant	Senior Leadership Reference	Sentiment
Tara	Male-Dominated, Old-Boys Club, All-White	"It started out as daunting." "I was very bothered initially." "There wasn't a chance for me to network because I did not smoke."
Renell	All-White, Male	"I had to prove myself."
Sheniqua	All-Black	"My male leader felt intimidated by me because I had an opinion. I was smarter, and he felt that his voice was not heard."

Participant	Senior Leadership Reference	Sentiment
Cynthia	All-White, Male	"I did not feel like I was understood." "I felt unsafe and could not say what came to mind or ask for support." "My struggles were brushed off." "Clients used racial slurs." "I have been fighting a battle." "As immigrants, we are overachievers and need to do everything in our power to get more opportunities."
Rita	All-White, Male	"I was recruited from outside, so I was not an old-timer." "I was told, 'You are a superstar, and we will see what you can do.' But I was constantly navigating organizational shift." "I was liked very much, but the work experience was exhausting." "Women are classified as having potential, and they try to give you opportunities. Men are just given the bigger opportunity because they are rising stars."
Serena	White and Asian, Male	"I felt on an island." "I felt like I was this street-smart person who entered Ivy League politics." "Imposter syndrome is tied to women and minorities, which puts the onus on them." "It is gaslighting."

Participant	Senior Leadership Reference	Sentiment
Diva	Diverse	"Inclusion is at the forefront." "I feel that women's representation is pretty equal." "It is more collaborative, where you could be in the room full of leaders and have an opinion or speak up."
Sima	All-White, Male	"In the technical field, it is very challenging when you are presenting, and there are ten men and one woman in the room." "If you speak candidly or express your opinion, ten others will disagree immediately or ignore you." "Hostile behavior continuously happens, and you feel demotivated, or you feel that your voice is not heard."
Jaya	Diverse but Could Do Better	"If I were a male coming in, regardless of skin color, I would be treated differently." "I am earning what the incumbent male in my position was earning three to four years ago." "I get very angry because there are minority women in my company who get paid very low." "The power you have in your role greatly affects how you are seen." "Power suppresses color."

Participant	Senior Leadership Reference	Sentiment
Chanell	Cis-Gendered, Caucasian, Male	"I don't see partners and directors with diverse backgrounds, which feels demoralizing." "It becomes difficult to believe I can see myself in a higher position." "Those of us with minority backgrounds face additional headwinds at mid-level management."
Sue	White, Male	"It is mainly White males. We don't shy away from this, and we are not proud of it. We acknowledge that we want to change this. In the last few years, senior leadership has seen much more diversity. It is a slow and steady evolution, and I am seeing a lot of improvement."
Maya	Diverse	"We have a strong diversity, equity, and inclusion program to give people of minority background opportunities to be more visible and get chances." "Within a week of my joining, the company announced a divestiture, and if you are a new hire, you might lose your job."
Jing	Caucasian, Male	"I am many degrees removed from a position at senior leadership level." "If diversity were to increase at director level in some way, it would be aspirational to mid-level managers hoping to expand and grow."

Participant	Senior Leadership Reference	Sentiment
Naomi	All-White	"When you are the only Black person in the room, you are conditioned not to speak up." "In retail, there may be leaders of color in stores. But when corporate walks through, everyone is 100 percent White, which is very noticeable." "You don't ever want to be labeled as a Black woman who is difficult, has a bad attitude, or is hard to work with. All those stereotypes you hear, you don't want that for yourself." "When your White coworkers have a bad day or get upset or cry at work, it is okay."

Table 3 shows an analysis of senior leadership representation and sentiments associated with being a minority woman. These also speak to challenges and struggles as a woman of color in mid-level management.

Three themes emerged from the narratives in Table 3, including minority women,

1. had to work harder to prove themselves,

2. faced additional challenges due to hostile behavior and occupational stereotypes, and

3. did not have the same advantages in terms of pay and opportunities compared to their male counterparts.

As you see in the narratives presented in Table 3, these experiences often lead to self-doubt and diminished confidence—subtle yet powerful effects commonly associated with gaslighting in the workplace.

Furthermore, in response to the question, "How diverse is the senior leadership in your organization, and what does it mean for you to be a minority woman in your current role?" there were nineteen references or excerpts from eleven women to male-dominated or predominantly White men and women in senior leadership positions resulting in negative sentiments, such as feeling demoralized, being unable to express opinions candidly without disagreements or hostile behavior, feeling daunted and frustrated when male counterparts were paid disproportionately more, being unable to network or socialize, and facing "additional headwinds." While many felt inequity and unfair treatment, some women felt that their company acknowledged these struggles, proactively provided minorities opportunities to grow, and focused on inclusion as a top priority. However, these findings indicate microaggressions and stereotypes that further perpetuate the glass ceiling.

The personal experiences of minority women shed light on a persistent problem—the systemic lack of fairness in promotion processes. While some individuals overcome these obstacles, far too many are held back by implicit bias, unclear criteria, and inconsistent practices. But what would fairness in promotions look like? In the next chapter, we explore the concept of justice in promotion processes, defining what equitable practices entail and how they can reshape workplace culture.

PART II

PROMOTION PROCESS

4
JUSTICE IN PROMOTIONS

JUSTICE REFERS TO the principle of moral rightness and the maintenance of what is just by law or fairness. In the context of the promotion process, justice reflects the perception that decisions are made through transparent, consistent, and ethical procedures that respect all individuals involved. Promotion justice goes beyond simply being fair—which implies impartiality and absence of bias—and extends to whether the process is equitable, meaning it accounts for individual needs, contributions, and barriers. While fairness treats everyone the same, and equity seeks to give people what they need to succeed, justice in promotion emphasizes whether the system produces outcomes that uphold integrity, merit, and respect. This chapter explores how organizations can cultivate justice in promotions to build trust, motivation, and long-term commitment among employees.

Employee perception of justice is a predictor of satisfaction with promotion outcomes. When researchers examined the role of justice in promotion decisions, they found that the greater the perception of fairness in the promotion process and decisions, the more employees were satisfied with their job and promotion opportunities. Perceived procedural justice is the best predictor of organizational outcomes, such as organizational commitment and turnover intentions. Also, when a supervisor or manager makes promotion decisions, perceived interactional justice is positively related to trust in the supervisor or manager, respectively.[42]

Despite strong incentives to promote from within, many minority employees—particularly those with long tenure and proven skills—are frequently overlooked in promotion and succession planning. This consistent pattern contributes to the high turnover of diverse talent across organizations. As discussed in Chapter 2: Revisioning DEI, there is a sharp decline in the number of minority women advancing at each stage of the promotion ladder, resulting in severe underrepresentation in senior leadership roles.

Additionally, the internal work climate plays a significant role in retention. When employees—especially women and people of color—are subjected to ongoing incivility or subtle exclusion, their intent to leave increases significantly. These patterns not only hinder advancement but also push capable individuals out of workplaces entirely.

Through interviews with minority women, I gained further insight into these trends—particularly the systemic and interpersonal barriers they encounter. Their stories reveal why many ultimately disengage from the promotion process or exit the workforce altogether.

Fair-Opportunity Framework

Fair opportunity in the promotion process means no person should receive a promotion, reward, or raise based on underserved or unjust advantages, and no person should be denied a promotion, reward, or raise based on undeserved disadvantages. When the fair-opportunity rule is applied in the workforce, and we can see fewer broad inequalities in the distribution of benefits based on effort, contribution, and merit, we can say that justice has been achieved.[43]

Promotion Justice

Historically, promotion ladders were classified by occupations, skills, training requirements, and gender. Although sex segregation of jobs and career lines may be less pervasive today, the results imply that gender was a powerful independent basis of clustering jobs in promotion ladders and of the position of jobs within those ladders.[44]

Political and institutional forces, both inside and outside of organizations, shape the opportunity structures, for example, by gender differentiation, the presence of professional groups, unions, and the institutional environment. Organizations continue to adopt merit-based practices and standardization of the reward allocation process to eliminate inequity. However, such processes may mask inequality in the distribution of rewards and may generate discrimination in the workplace.[45]

The situation of justice is present in the process of internal promotion when a person is due benefits through merit or burden because of their properties or circumstances. Therefore, injustice involves wrongful acts or omissions that deny people benefits to which they have a right or the failure to distribute the burdens fairly.[43]

Distributive justice in the promotion and reward process is the fair, equitable, and appropriate distribution of rewards and raises. Its scope includes HR policies concerning diversity and burdens related to the promotion process, such as privileges and opportunities based on race, gender, ethnicity, IQ, accent, national origin, and social status. These aspects of a person's identity are often irrelevant and introduce discriminatory treatment based on differences for which affected individuals are not responsible.[43] Hence, it's essential to introduce a fair-opportunity rule that attempts to eliminate or reduce unjust forms of distribution.

Existing research on promotions states that individuals are identified for career advancement based on performance, personal characteristics, favoritism, or luck.[46] Relationships with mentors, managers, and other organizations, as well as social networks, make the individuals aware of the promotion opportunities and are a source of recommendations or references for applicants.[47] When job announcements are informal, word-of-mouth recruitment networks are essential.

In 2020, 45 percent of the participants in the federal government reported benefiting from information gained from networking in professional development.[12] Minority employees have a lower perception of the usefulness of their career networks, hesitate to utilize them, and expect rejection or fear of conforming to the stereotypical expectation of incompetency.[48] Moreover, in predominantly White organizations, social networks are racially segregated, which causes difficulty for minority groups to secure employment.[49,50]

Well-educated Black executives who experienced discrimination in white-collar employment face "triple jeopardy" due to simultaneously being Black, solo, and a token, resulting in a bias in job entry and performance evaluation. Prejudice due to "attribution error" continues to be a significant barrier to occupational attainment for the Black community. Due to frustration, top job performance becomes difficult because of the stereotyped explanation of Black behavior as "bad" by White counterparts.[50] Another term that emerged in 2020 through studies on Asian Americans and their experiences with workplace discrimination is the "bamboo ceiling," which prevents Asian Americans from advancement into leadership positions due to the model minority myth.[51] The model minority myth is a stereotype that portrays certain minority groups—most commonly Asian Americans—as uniformly successful, particularly in education, income, and behavior. While it may appear positive on the surface, this narrative is harmful because it erases the diversity of experiences within the group, places immense pressure to meet unrealistic expectations, and is often used to downplay systemic racism or invalidate the struggles of other marginalized communities. It can also silence the voices of those within the so-called "model" group who face barriers or discrimination. In comparison to this study, the 2016 National Asian American Survey (N = 1,013) identified a high degree of perceived discrimination in denied promotion decisions due to disadvantages among Asian women.

Organizational factors also play a role in the promotion decision process, including a tendency to promote from within to reduce cost, increase longevity within the same company, and reduce staff turnover. While promoting from within fosters a feeling of gratitude and allows for developing a trusted relationship with superiors, it may also create unwanted competition and negative emotions among members in response to being passed up for promotions, which disrupts team functioning.[43]

Job advancement comes with positive emotions and job satisfaction but can lead to negative feelings or anxiety due to uncertainty.[52] How employees react to promotions relates to their differences and perception of justice or fairness. Whether an individual perceives fairness as procedural depends on their level of trust and commitment. There has been a greater emphasis on the roles of justice and fairness perception. The perception was that the promotion of members of the opposite gender was less fair than those of the same gender.[53, 54] Internal promotions create a feeling of inequity in those who do not receive a promotion and make some individuals unwilling to surrender to the authority of their newly promoted peers.[47]

▶ My Findings on Promotion Justice

Women I talked to were explicitly asked about whether they felt that the promotion process was fair or equitable. Patterns and themes derived from the women's responses to the questions (shown in Table 4), "Do you think you were treated fairly? Do you think the decision had to do with your demographics? Do you think there is a subjective bias in the promotion decision-making process?"

Table 4

Participant Responses to whether they were treated fairly

	Yes	No	Maybe	No Response	Percentage of Yes/ Maybe
Do you think you were treated fairly?	9	4	1	0	71
Do you think the decision had to do with your demographics?	4	8	1	1	36
Having gone through the promotion process, do you believe there is subjective bias in the process?	13	1	0	0	93

Table 4 displays the analysis of responses to questions that answer question "Do minority women find the promotion process at their workplaces fair or equitable?" Seventy-one percent of (ten) the women I interviewed felt that they were treated fairly through their promotion experience, 36 percent (four) attributed the decision-making to their demographics, and 93 percent (thirteen) felt that there was subjective bias in the decision-making process.

▶ Factors that Contribute to the Perception of Promotion Justice

The narrative from the stories below highlights their response to question "What specific attributes of their experience contribute to their perception?" This section includes factors the women attributed to subjective bias in the promotion decision-making. This section also provides further insight into the promotion decision-making process and the women's perceptions of managers' biases, which may have influenced the actual promotion decision-making. Last, it captures changes in the women's perspectives after a promotion cycle.

Women who received the promotion perceived fair treatment (distributive justice), and those who did not receive the promotion questioned the decision-making process (procedural justice), supporting existing research.[55] Four women felt that they were not fairly treated attributed that treatment to demographic inequities—mainly gender and race—in the promotion decision-making or allocation of raises.

Tara said with certainty that demographics, such as age, gender, and race, sometimes play a role in promotion decision-making. In her case, pregnancy may also have been a factor, as her manager told her that the company needed to fill the position immediately and had someone with experience in mind. She was informally screened by the hiring manager and denied a chance for a formal interview with a panel, which Tara realized when everyone on the panel did not show up for the interview other than the hiring manager. This made her feel deceived. Furthermore, she only learned about the position (with its requisition number) because it was announced in a team meeting. Also, the hiring portal did not allow applicants to view the open positions' team or hiring manager. Hence, biases could be attributed to a lack of transparency and inconsistencies in the promotion process and demographics.

Rita was ambivalent in her response. She did not feel that she was treated unfairly, but she did feel that she was taken for granted. Although her company did not have a policy that new hires could not be promoted within a specific time frame after hire, she was not promoted primarily because one person thought she was too new. She shared,

> I don't think they would have taken a White man for granted. If there are two people with the skills, capabilities, and potential on an accelerated path, and one of them is a White man, they will treat him much more carefully. I think my gender and my race made it easier for them to assume that I would just stick around. I don't think they expect women to take control of their careers, to negotiate for themselves, and to make the moves that need to be made as quickly as men will make them. Women generally tend to use the language, "I am grateful for what I have." Women are expected to be happy with what they have been given. Men are expected to ask for more and negotiate for more.

Rita attributed negative promotion outcomes to rigid company policy and racial and gender stereotypes.

Although Renell did not think her demographics had anything to do with the promotion decision-making, she said, "Having a good relationship with the people that were the decision makers definitely helped." From her perspective, she was treated fairly. However, she could see why it may not be fair from the perspective of other candidates or the interviewing manager and his team because the hiring manager's manager told them that she should be promoted. She reported that the hiring manager's manager had a subjective bias because he knew her personally, and they had a rapport, which prevented him from making an objective decision. From the Renell's point of view,

> My manager could argue that even if I was looking at it objectively because I know her, I know she can do X, Y, and Z; she has been doing those things and is qualified. On the other hand, the hiring manager and his favorites on the team also had a subjective bias about who they thought should be in the role because they knew the other candidate. Ultimately, it is about who is more powerful to make the decision.

Renell agreed that the outcome favors individuals with familiarity, relational, and experiential context with the decision-maker and those in a position of power.

Serena believed she was treated unfairly and that the system was designed to allow managers to favor their friends or people they like and people they want to keep around. Her perception of just treatment resulted from being friends with the decision-makers. She gave an example of three White men who were exceptions and were hired at the same level as her but were quickly promoted to head of the industry. From her perspective, "They were White men who went to the same schools as the people in charge. They are more likable; they don't make people uncomfortable, and they do not challenge anybody." Hence, the reasons attributed to subjective bias in decision-making were, "The manager likes you, you are like the manager, and you are White."

Sima reported that she was treated fairly through the interview process and was promoted but was not given a raise because her managers knew she was "hungry for growth, and she would accept it." There was also no initial change in her grade level. However, there was a significant increase in responsibility. She initially interviewed for a position with a team of twenty-two in one country, and with customer demand, the team grew to forty-five in two countries and two time zones. She was still not rewarded for a position for which the company would have needed three leaders in three time zones. She also reported that the leaders developed goals at the beginning of the year but did not help employees see them through. Based on Sima's experience, promotions are not dependent on achieving the goals or performing above and beyond. According to her, some factors that negatively impact the promotion outcome include layoffs, restructuring, lack of visibility with the new leaders/managers, and lack of availability of promotional positions.

Jaya reported that her demographics did not play a role in the promotion decision-making because the company needed her for the role to which she was promoted. However, she reported a subjective bias and pay inequity when promoted. She was not questioned because she met the hiring manager's criteria: "someone who knew the technology, the business, and the people around." Although she had the same or more responsibilities and had proven success in her performance, her current compensation was nowhere close to what the previous male incumbent was making three to four years before. She reported feeling pressure to prove herself and work harder than her White male counterparts.

Themes that emerged from the responses from the women who felt there is subjective bias in the promotion decision-making include:

1. Affinity bias

2. Rigid HR policies, particularly capping promotion rates, meeting diversity quotas, creating positions with specific individuals in mind, tying eligibility for promotion to a timeframe based on the date of employment

3. microaggressions or discrimination.

Cynthia reported that the supervisor forgot about the interview when she first applied for a promotion. While she was waiting, the supervisor came out and said, "I already know who's going to get this job. But if you want to apply for this other job, you are more than welcome." Hence, in her experience, positions are often created with one person in mind and are posted knowing who will get the job. The application process is simply a formality. She shared another example wherein an external candidate who was well-qualified and had more experience than an internal candidate was not hired because the manager knew the internal candidate they wanted for the position.

Chanell felt that because her position was unique and did not have a generic career path, she had to do more self-advocacy than those promoted with minimal effort. In her experience:

The company recruits from certain schools and majors, and because I was not part of this affinity circle, i.e., same university, I am not White, and not a male, I am not being told, "Let me get you promoted." Those who have been in that affinity circle will get promoted after one year, switch teams after one year, and get promoted to the next level.

When she spoke up and confronted the manager, she was told it would take two years to be considered for a promotion. She attested to the affinity bias and stated that individuals who have the same demographics and similar backgrounds get more attention.

Jing also felt there may be some bias because most positions she interviewed for have gone to individuals within teams because they have established relationships with the decision-makers. She reported, "If they are comparing my performance versus their performance, they have much more familiarity with the person, and this person knows the future responsibilities that the role would take on."

Diva and Sue perceived subjective bias in the performance evaluation process, which includes calibration by all the team directors to gain consensus on their final rating. The rating is based on competencies, and the raise is based on the rating. Diva pointed out a performance management policy whereby not everyone can get an "outstanding" or "exceeds expectations" rating. "Companies want to keep a bell curve in the performance rating where 5 percent needs to get outstanding, 5 percent gets the lowest rating, and everybody else just fits in the middle." One drawback she shared was a lack of visibility of her work with her manager.

Sue felt there is subjective bias in consensus building for performance rating, and there is also objective evaluation of individuals' performance, and both are necessary for promotion decision-making. In her company, individuals are each assigned a career advisor, and promotability depends on the leaders. According to her, it is okay for leaders to be subjective if they support and advocate for the employee.

Naomi attributed the subjective bias to microaggression and discrimination based on skin color. She gave an example of a Latina woman promoted because of her fair skin. She heard from a third party that the hiring manager would "not even look at her." Naomi shared another experience where the manager claimed to be an ally for diversity.

When I interviewed for a different program, the hiring manager said, "I think you would be so happy to know that we have a diverse group, and you are going to love to get to know all these diverse people." She (a White woman with blond hair and blue eyes) was so pleased with herself that she found all these diverse people from different ethnic backgrounds. She did not do anything special to recruit us. We are everywhere, especially in big cities.

This perspective indicates a belief that managers and leaders frequently promote individuals to meet their diversity quota and portray a scarcity of diverse talent.

All ten women who reported being treated fairly also reported having "good working relationships" and "rapport" with their managers. They reported that their manager was "open and transparent" and was "supportive" of their career advancement. Two women (Sheniqua and Diva) who experienced a standard job posting process, interviews, and selection were also among the individuals who reported being treated fairly. Two women (Chanell and Sue) selected for promotion based on their performance also felt they were treated fairly.

Having gone through a promotion experience, women were asked, "Has this changed your perspective about the organization's position on career advancement for minorities?" Six of them reported feeling more positive and hopeful about future advancement for minority women. Tara attributed this to a greater focus on different movements for minorities in the last few years and on hiring more women and people of color in leadership roles. Diva said there is more awareness, and open positions related to diversity and inclusion are announced in a weekly e-mail from the diversity and inclusion group to the whole company. Naomi reported feeling that the company is moving in the right direction by making efforts to support minorities, celebrate different cultures, and focus on hiring more minority women in leadership roles.

While justice in promotions is the goal, the reality for many minority women is far from equitable. Promotions are often marred by subjective decision-making, unspoken expectations, and systemic barriers that disproportionately impact underrepresented groups. Understanding these inequities in detail is crucial for identifying where the breakdown occurs and what must be done to address it. The next chapter takes a closer look at the root causes of these imbalances and their far-reaching effects.

5
INEQUITIES IN PROMOTIONS

CURRENT RESEARCH ON promotion and promotion decision-making shows that most companies use a performance appraisal process to evaluate employee competencies and abilities to fulfill their current job duties and responsibilities. While this is intended to be a standardized process, research shows that bias, favoritism, and inequities persist regarding salary growth, rewards, and promotion decision-making. Adopting a fair-opportunity framework can help eliminate unjust advantages based on personal characteristics, provide equal opportunity, and promote just practices within the workplace.

Merit-Based Promotions

Merit-based promotions lack objectivity in decision-making because of the subjective nature of performance evaluations. Although performance evaluation policies are often adopted to motivate employees and ensure meritocracy, policies with limited transparency and accountability increase performance-reward bias and reduce equity in the workplace.[45]

Although several organizations claim that they make employee salary growth and promotion decisions based on merit and performance evaluations and that it is a fair and legitimate process, empirical studies have found that demographic inequality persists even with the adoption of merit-based practices.[56]

Once merit is measured through the appraisal process, women and minority employees still receive different rewards for the same merit scores as White men (after controlling for the job, work unit, supervisor, and other relevant human capital characteristics).[45] Biases across multiple stages of employment can create a further disadvantage for minority women as it relates to promotions and monetary or non-monetary reward decisions. Hence, it is essential to have a common and usable understanding of merit for all employees, managers, and executives so merit is understood and applied consistently and fairly in employment decisions that impact the careers of individuals within organizations that aim to be meritocratic.[56] To make the promotion process fair, it is imperative to obtain the perspectives of those being considered for promotions and evaluate any inequities or barriers to seeking promotion.

The hope is, these realities and stories will enhance managers' understanding of perceptions of minority women as they relate to merit evaluations, salary growth, and promotions. Managers can address these perceptions and reduce or eliminate the barriers experienced by minority women. This book also uncovers salient features in the leader-member relationship that will help or hinder employee growth and considerations for promotions and/or rewards. Employees who perceive inequities will be able to examine their perceptions and understand the consequences of their actions to obtain practical tools and tips on advancing in the workplace, irrespective of race or gender.

Promotion and Reward Process

Pay-for-performance and performance-management systems measure and reward employees' merit and contributions to the company.[45] The job promotion process enables organizations to find the best talent within the company to fill more senior positions, and it allows employees to advance their careers within the company.[57]

Promoting high-performing employees to leadership positions is customary based on a performance appraisal at the end of a performance-management cycle. Certain organizations also use mid-year evaluations for promotion opportunities. Offering a promotion is a strategy for employee development, a reward for superior performance, or recognition of employee capabilities.[58]

Use of Assessment Tools

Companies use assessment tools to hire and develop talent, identify and train emerging leaders, evaluate performance to make promotion and reward decisions, and understand unique skills, abilities, behaviors, and traits.

Assessments provide objective feedback that helps candidates enhance self-awareness, which enables personal and professional growth. Assessments yield diverse effects on performance across different practices. Assessment tools operationalize the desired knowledge when compared to interview-based verbal evaluations.[59]

Various assessment tools are available in the market, including personality-based, behavior-based, competency-based, and so on. Moreover, using a multi-trait, multi-method

(MTMM) approach to assess an individual's potential provides unique variance better than performance alone in determining the promotability that can inform talent management decisions.[60]

Based on this research, organizations would do well to choose the appropriate tool for assessment based on validity, reliability, and established norms. Careful selection involves choosing a tool based on what it is intended to measure and what population is being studied to ensure appropriate application, especially when using such tools to promote minority groups.

Impact of Internal Promotions on Teams

Promotion involves mobility between units, teams, and even across geographic boundaries to provide an individual with greater responsibility, higher status, and a better salary.[61] This requires learning new norms and cultural practices, adapting to new work rules, and building relationships with new colleagues. Organizations often provide resources to support a smooth transition. This poses challenges for newly promoted individuals and those left behind, such as learning how to manage former peers and managing one's changed identity, which often involves a shift in work relationships and a change in how one is perceived by peers.

On one hand, it may give team members a promotion advantage. For example, the newly appointed team leader may effectively advocate for the team to senior leadership and across departments. If promoted to a different department or team, the leader may influence the former team positively by providing resources and management advice.[62] For a leader with well-established relationships, building trust and obtaining cooperation may be easier.

On the other hand, the situation may create interpersonal challenges for the team, resulting in a promotion penalty. If team members are jealous, angry, or feel betrayed by the internal promotion, this sense of injustice can harm group cohesiveness.[63] Those passed over for promotion often attribute this to the ill-intentions of others within the organization—either peers or decision-makers—and may believe that the promotion decision was not based on merit.[64] These individuals may also reason that their former peers solicited a promotion for themselves by keeping it from the teams' knowledge, or the promotion was offered outside of formal channels. The chapter "Trust in the Context of Performance Appraisal" (2011) in the book *Trust and Human Resource Management*[47] states the following:

> In the minds of the teammates, there may be advantages to having a friend in a position of power (a spokesperson), but at the same time, promotions create psychological distance and lower trust, as well as fears about divided loyalties (management versus team), all of which may engender envy and resentment over the peer's success.

Overall, research suggests the detrimental effects of internal promotion outweigh the evidence of beneficial effects.

Furthermore, trust plays a critical role in determining the success of internal promotions within workgroups. Studies show that a leader promoted from within the team is more accepted than an external leader. Trust facilitates cooperation in the group, positive expectations, and a perception of benevolence. Trust also allows for information sharing between members of the group without worry that the information will be used against them. In addition to vertical growth and promotion to a higher position, lateral transfer is an aspect of

internal mobility that may also meet an individual's require-
ment for a job change.[47]

Organizations often provide formal training, mentorship,
or career enhancement opportunities to individuals before an
actual job change to prepare for growth and reap the benefit of
employee retention. Employees often view skill enhancement
opportunities (e.g., training, certification, etc.) as benefits.
Internal promotions can significantly impact turnover and
retention, and multiple measures recommended above can
be of value to an organization.[65]

What Did Women Say About the Promotion Process?

▶ Application Process

This section includes patterns and trends in responses to questions about the job application process. I asked them how did
the participants find out about the position? Was the position
posted? Did they interview for it? What prompted them to
apply? Were they ready for it? How did their manager take
their decision to apply?

Based on the interviews, it was clear that many companies did not have a standardized promotion process by
which all employees had a common usable understanding of
the promotion process. Exceptions included one large-scale
pharmaceutical company, one small family-owned non-profit
company, and a large technology company. Table 5 shows
whether the positions were posted or announced internally,
whether the women were formally interviewed, and whether
the positions were created specifically for individuals as part
of their career development.

Table 5

Application Process

Application Process	Number of Participants
Position posted	9
Announced internally within the team	7
A standardized process where positions were posted, and there were formal interviews	3
Interviewed just for formality	5
No interview and no posting of the position, which was created as part of their career development plan	5

Of the five individuals who reported that the interview was a formality, two women reported not receiving the position because management already had another person in mind. Three other positions were created for the women as part of their career development plan. Five women did not receive an interview, nor were the positions posted because they were created as part of their career development plan, meaning eight positions were created for specific individuals.

Nine women who were promoted reported feeling that they were ready because they were already performing at a higher level. Other reasons for readiness included being confident that they could perform the job, knowing the expectations of the position, speaking with others in the role, and having their team's support. Three of the women felt they were not ready for promotions when they had the opportunity because of personal reasons, such as pregnancy and family obligations during the COVID-19 pandemic.

Twelve women reported that their manager was transparent about the open position and supported the promotion. One felt they were hired at a much lower level than their experience, and it took years for them to attain the level for which the promotion was possible. The manager of one of the women felt that it was too soon for the employee to be promoted because it had only been a few months since they were hired at the company.

Promotion inequalities are not random; they stem from decision-making processes that are often opaque, inconsistent, and influenced by bias. Whether intentional or not, these decisions shape careers and reinforce systemic disparities. To dismantle these barriers, we must unpack how promotion decisions are made, who is involved, and what factors influence the outcomes. The following chapter examines these processes in depth, revealing critical insights into how they can be improved.

6
DECISION-MAKING FOR PROMOTIONS

Social Connectedness

I HAVE ALSO tried to inquire about the relationship between women seeking promotion and their managers and their impact on promotion outcomes. The nature of the relationship with the leader may cause division of members into those who are in-group, whose beliefs align with the leader, and those who are out-group, whose values do not align with the leader. The disadvantaged groups will accept their situation if the intergroup situation is stable and perceived as legitimate.[66] If there is a small proportion of minorities in a team or a group, it does not lead to collectivistic action to advocate for procedural changes. It likely leads to individual acts of speaking up, which do not gain the necessary momentum to make systemic change.

Those who romanticize the leader tend to form one group, and those with divergent thinking and those who speak up and challenge the leader form another. Members of this second group may not be appreciated if the leader is not inclusive and open to feedback and does not always yield positive results.[67] In my inquiry, I have delved deeper into this leader-member exchange relationship to examine discrimination, vulnerability, and exploitation experienced by minorities.

Furthermore, employee socialization experiences that allow social interactions and relationship building generally do not include activities that interest a wide pool of participants or encourage the participation of employees with diverse backgrounds. Some employees may prefer structured activities, such as advocating for a social cause or a charitable activity. I hope to find such potential solutions by engaging the employees to obtain their perspective.

There is little research on the effects of social connectedness or manager-employee relationship and personnel promotion. The findings from my research uncover this relationship and how it impacts promotions and the rewards process. The interview included specific questions about the leader-follower relationship, such as employee perception of trust, social connectedness, and managers' confidence in their abilities to succeed in the new position. The women I interviewed shared the in-group and out-group dynamics among the team and how it influences promotion decision-making.

The nature of the relationship between the employee and their manager is key to promotion decision-making. According to the Leader-Member Exchange (LMX) theory, effective leadership occurs when leaders and followers maintain a high-quality exchange relationship with a high degree of mutual trust, respect, and obligation.[1,68] Leaders should develop high-quality exchanges with all subordinates, thus making the entire work unit an "in-group." Leaders and followers experience a high-quality LMX relationship if there is respect and they enjoy working with each other.[1]

LMX theory presumes that leaders do not treat every subordinate the same, that LMX quality can range from low to high, and that members' work-related attitudes and behaviors depend on how their leaders treat them and how high this relationship quality is.[69] Employees with a high LMX perform well because they can exchange resources with the leader and benefit from leniency bias.[70] A positive LMX relationship makes the employee feel comfortable to reach out to the leader, provides easy access to the leader, and enables opportunities for the employee to learn from the leader through observation. Guidance, exposure, protection, and friendship provided by mentors are the strongest predictors of promotion.[35] However, there is also contradictory research that shows interpersonal factors, such as friendliness, do not affect supervisor performance ratings as strongly as ability, knowledge, and proficiency.[71] Employees who can create the image or reputation of being essential to the success of the unit or group make the leader come across as more effective, and it is natural for the leader to give them a positive performance rating. Thus, leaders' perception of an employee is important and influential within the organization and positively linked to their evaluation of the employee's performance.[70] LMX, therefore, offers a key paradigm for understanding implicit bias in promotions.

Decision-Making Biases and Promotability

Leaders must be aware of their perceptions and biases while making promotion decisions and look for skills, abilities, and knowledge rather than solely basing the promotion decision on liking, similarities in personality, or a high LMX relationship. Performance evaluations and ratings are principal factors in making career decisions. Because an objective performance evaluation is difficult, biased perceptions of promotion decision-makers may prove risky for organizations.

Organizations should monitor individuals to avoid bias in their decision-making and implement countermeasures, such as instituting committees for checks and balances and providing clear decision criteria to reduce room for subjective interpretation and biases.

For promotion decision-makers, the promotion reaches beyond the employee's rating and considers how the employee got there. What perceived virtues do supervisors ascribe to those they promote? Decision-makers associate success with factors tied to effort more than ability, such as conscientiousness, job dedication, and an initiative-taking personality. They perceived higher levels of these factors in those with upward performance trends, even if their performance levels had not reached the level of others.[72,73] Moreover, the studies showed that performance change is vital for promotion regardless of employee gender. The gender of the decision-maker also does not seem to influence decisions for promoting employees.[4,74] These studies suggest that behaviors that show dedication and commitment are more important than ability and gender for promotion decision-makers.

A well-designed process for deciding which employee receives a promotion is crucial to minimize the perception of injustice and reduce negative effects, such as low employee motivation and premature resignation. Selection of the right individuals for succession planning can allow for talent flow to the highest levels of the organization, resulting in the greatest impact. Individuals with high-performance ratings do not necessarily receive high-promotability ratings.

A study done in 2011 examined a model for the promotion process involving district managers being considered for advancement to the position of regional manager in a large organization. Using data from multiple sources (for example, employees, immediate supervisors, personnel files, and task forces charged with succession planning), the researcher found that a district manager's past performance, current job tenure, and prior job tenure predict the manager's promotability rating, which, in turn, predicts whether the manager is promoted. Biases can impact the manager's perception of an individual's abilities and influence the promotion decision. Individuals with longer tenure are typically older, and the organization's decision-maker may be less likely to promote them even if they have the capability because they are nearing retirement. On the contrary, those who have mastered the skills in a shorter tenure and have a previous history of rapid promotion are considered and perceived as having high potential and the right characteristics for advancement.[75] Hence, factors that dictate the strength of this promotability rating include:

1. The manager's perception of individuals' capability and motivation

2. The similarity of the job the individual currently holds to the job they would be promoted to

3. Whether the individual declines the promotion due to personal preferences (e.g., need to travel, relocate, and work long or random hours[76]

Another study in the same year identified five key determinants used by managers in making managerial promotion decisions:

1. Image/substance

2. Hygiene factors

3. Fit

4. Organizational tenure

5. Cost-benefit analysis/difficulty of change[77]

We have already examined the effects of tenure and promotability and the financial implications of hiring from outside the organization. We will now explore the impact of image and reputation management.

Liking an individual is positively correlated with promotability. People prefer to connect and interact with those whom they can identify with culturally and those they perceive to be like them. It is easier to establish rapport and predict behavior. Hence, the dominant group's norms, values, rules, and policies reflect its values and cultural biases, which can conflict with those of the minority group. In addition, the cognitive biases of individual decision-makers may also influence the promotion decision-making process.[8] For example, decision-makers may have preconceived notions, such as women lacking the traits appropriate for effective management, succeeding because of luck, not devoting themselves fully because of family obligations, or lacking commitment.[4,78]

Promotion decision-makers choose candidates with whom they feel comfortable and use systematically different criteria for promoting people based on gender.[8]

Promotion Allocation

Promotions are vital to the success of the organization and can be implemented by using:

1. Merit-based systems: Candidates are ranked according to performance, and the highest-ranked candidates are promoted.

2. Seniority-based systems: Candidates most experienced in the job, industry, or organization are promoted.

3. Random systems: Candidates are selected based on random chance rather than performance or seniority.

Those promoted based on merit experience more satisfaction than those promoted based on seniority. While merit-based promotion is associated with high employee satisfaction, seniority-based promotions can help maintain workplace harmony and eliminate unfair selection due to favoritism.[61]

Random allocation of promotions often occurs as part of an organizational restructuring; ad-hoc promotions are granted to fulfill the business needs or to retain top performers. Internal promotion helps provide a sense of job security for those who feel ready to take on additional responsibilities. There is a positive relationship between job promotion practices and the perceived performance of employees. Hence, providing fair promotion opportunities will typically enhance employees' performance and commitment to the organization.

▶ Promotion Outcome: What Helped and Hindered?

This section outlines the themes of the responses from women who received the promotion for which they applied versus those who did not. Most of the women reported that the biggest hindrance to a positive promotion outcome was a lack of visibility with skip-level management or senior leadership, particularly due to the reorganization, divestitures, and restructuring of the company, which happened every two to three years, resulting in significant leadership and management turnover.

Others attributed their lack of promotion to rigid HR policies, such as a limited quota for promotions and hiring individuals at levels below their established experience, lengthening their time to promotability within the organization (Serena); a rigid manager's belief that they were not ready for promotion because they had held their current position for only a few months and had to be at the company for least five years to be considered for promotion (Rita); the need to open a different location to provide a new experience to the applicant, which the manager considered important for a promotion (Naomi); and wanting someone immediately in the role when the participants were pregnant (Tara and Serena).

Jing attributed a negative outcome to personal factors, such as having a specialized niche or experience that does not match the opportunities that arise, leading cross-functional projects where they manage others' work but are not able to show that they manage direct reports, or not having an opportunity to show leadership skills. Diva reported delaying promotion due to balancing personal priorities, such as childcare and family responsibilities, with work during the COVID-19 pandemic, validating the McKinsey & Company 2021 report.[19]

Women who received the promotion attributed the positive outcome to their managers' or supervisors' support and encouragement. They reported having an open and transparent relationship with their supervisor. Six of them who did not get the promotion reported that the individual who received the promotion had more experience or tenure than them. Four of the women who got the position reported that they were promoted at the same grade level or with no pay increase; the appropriate title and salary were received a few years later. Three of them reported success in getting the promotion because of the recommendations and respect they received by collaborating with other managers in different departments. Chanell reported that in her organization, promotion decisions typically are based on senior leadership consensus and a vote.

These findings indicate that various factors help and hinder promotion outcomes. Hence, the interventions also need to focus on all levels of the organization, starting with HR policies and practices, managers' behaviors, and employees themselves to reduce bias and create equity in allocating promotions.

While history provides important context, the voices of those directly impacted bring these issues to life. The experiences of minority women navigating today's workplaces reveal the personal and professional toll of inequities. These stories offer a unique window into how systemic barriers manifest in real time and the resilience and strategies these women employ to move forward. In the next chapter, we turn to the participants themselves, hearing their perspectives and learning from their journeys.

PART III

ADVANCING FAIR OPPORTUNITIES

7
WHAT DRIVES PROMOTABILITY

What Does Company Value?

THIS SECTION INCLUDES an analysis of women's experiences regarding one or more actual promotions for which they applied. As described in Chapter 6, current literature alludes to the allocation of promotions based on merit, seniority, and random allocation of promotions.[61]

Information from interviews support this research, as three of the women reported that their performance primarily drove their promotion, and four women mentioned the significance of tenure and experience in receiving their promotions. In addition, interviews made clear that companies requiring special skills value experience, as two of the women were not granted a promotion because they had a shorter tenure even though they had mastered the desired skills. On the contrary, some companies do not promote individuals with tenure if they are nearing retirement.[75] This indicates that several other factors affect promotion decision-making that can fall under the category of random allocation.

Responses provided by the women to the question, "In your experience, what does your company seem to value based on who they promote? For example, performance, qualifications, experience, relationships, social network, etc.," are grouped into four categories or themes, which together are referred to as the promotability index. The promotability index is defined as a list of factors that were coined that serve to indicate the values or qualities that increase the likelihood of promotion. These were grouped into four categories, as shown below:

1. Company value

2. Networking or relationship building

3. Impression management

4. Promotability behaviors

The responses to company value showed an even distribution of performance, experience, knowledge, tenure, and qualification, as seen under the company value/index.

Figure 1

Promotability Index: Factors that Create Promotability

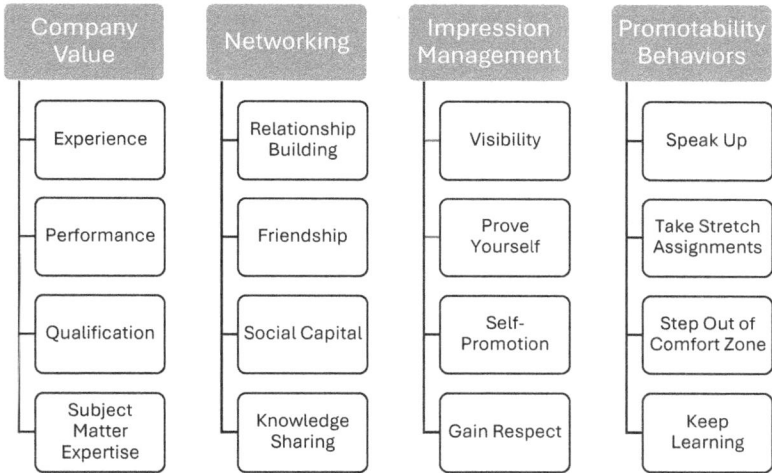

Company Value	Networking	Impression Management	Promotability Behaviors
Experience	Relationship Building	Visibility	Speak Up
Performance	Friendship	Prove Yourself	Take Stretch Assignments
Qualification	Social Capital	Self-Promotion	Step Out of Comfort Zone
Subject Matter Expertise	Knowledge Sharing	Gain Respect	Keep Learning

Networking and Relationship Building

Ten women highlighted the importance of networking and relationship building in increasing one's chances of getting promoted. This supports my assumption that social connectedness and social and cultural familiarity between leader and follower facilitate the promotion process.

Existing research on social connectedness included the impact of social networks, influence tactics or upward impression management from subordinates, and favorability and similarities with the manager, which directly validates the findings from this research, as shown in Table 6.

Table 6

What Companies Value in Promotion Decision-Making

Promotability Index	Reference to Specific Words	Number of Participants	Number of References
Company Value	Experience	4	4
	Performance	3	6
	Subject Matter Expertise	2	4
	Qualification	2	2
	Tenure	1	2
	Customer	1	2
	People First	1	1
	Community	1	1
	Inclusive	1	1
	Value-Driven Projects	1	1
	Innovation	1	1
	Collaboration	1	1
Networking and Relationship Building	Networking and Relationship	8	19
	Friends	2	2
	Social Capital	1	1
	Knowledge Sharing	1	1
Impression Management	Visibility	7	10
	Prove Yourself	4	5
	Self-Promotion	2	9
	Others Respect and Look Up to You	2	2

Promotability Index	Reference to Specific Words	Number of Participants	Number of References
	Nominate	1	2
	Good Face for the Public	1	1
	Represent Company Well	1	1
	Camera-Ready and Articulate	1	1
Promotability Behaviors	Speak Up	3	4
	Take Stretch Assignments	3	3
	Step Out of Comfort Zone	2	3
	Keep Learning	2	2
	Agility	1	1
	Be Authentic	1	1
	Be Courageous	1	1
	Emotional Intelligence	1	1
	Manage High-Stakes Situation	1	1
	Perseverance	1	1
	Resilience	1	1
	Smart	1	1
	Take Small Steps	1	1
	Volunteering	1	1
	Multiple Skill Sets	1	1

Impression Management: Influence Tactics

▶ Self-Promotion

Promoting oneself is a method to impress upon the leader one's strengths, contributions, and accomplishments. This is likely to impress leaders who are instrumental and exploitative because similarities (i.e., those who look like them or have similar cultural, social, and religious preferences) attract, resulting in high LMX.[70] It is crucial to remember that self-promotion does not always impress all observers, and whether it is a useful way to present oneself may depend on to whom one is trying to make a good impression.

Employees project confidence when they may not internally feel confident in their decision or may not be making the right decision to impress the leader. However, research shows no significant correlation between employee self-promotion and rewards, raises, promotions, or leaders' performance assessment.[79] When used too often or in annoying ways, self-promotion tactics will be less liked by the manager and given a low-performance appraisal.[2] An outcome such as a pay increase or job promotion may depend more on a subordinate's actual skills and performance than on using self-promotion tactics to focus attention on these qualifications.[2]

▶ Ingratiation

The use of influence tactics, such as ingratiation with flattery and deliberate effort to help, encourages positive relationships and fosters reciprocity. Moreover, political skills influence tactics such that the interaction can be related to supervisors' liking and can influence an individual's promotability.[39] Hence, increasing employee awareness about using gendered influence tactics and political skills can be linked to promotion success. Moreover, sincere ingratiation can increase how much the manager likes a subordinate and may also improve appraisals of subordinate performance.[2]

❱ Politicking

Political skill refers to "the ability to effectively understand others at work and to use such knowledge to influence others in ways that enhance one's personal and/or organizational objectives."[80]

Careerists gain promotion by creating an impression through deceit and politicking. They receive promotions and earn more money than non-careerists.[81] This can cause resentment among peers and supervisors as they may feel manipulated for personal gain. Such opportunistic orientation makes quick advancements but leaves chaos and conflict behind because individuals often cannot demonstrate substantial ability or skills to function effectively in their new senior role.[82]

Twelve of the women identified the importance of making an impression on the decision-makers and increasing one's visibility among senior leaders. In addition, they indicated specific promotability behaviors or individual attributes that they believe increased their promotability rating (see Table 6). Hence, the findings also support the research on image/substance as a key determinant in managerial promotion decisions (grouped in Table 6 as impression management), a factor referenced by at least half of the women.

As stated previously, research shows no significant correlation between employee self-promotion and rewards, raises, promotions, or leaders' performance assessment.[79] My conclusion does not fully align with past research in this way, as at least two of the women highlighted the importance of self-promotion and self-advocacy. Taking on additional responsibilities and stretch assignments (three of the women) and gaining visibility (seven of the women) can also be actions for promoting oneself.

Self-promotion for career advancements allowed the women to:

1. Build a personal brand that involved identifying their unique strengths, values, and expertise and communicating them to others

2. Actively participate in events to get noticed and engage in meaningful conversations with colleagues and mentors

3. Highlight their accomplishments and showcase their contributions to supervisors and senior leaders by sharing progress reports, presenting in meetings, and volunteering for high-visibility projects

4. Speak up or advocate for self, articulate ideas, and express ambitions and goals

Specific Promotability Behaviors Shared by the Women

In this section, let's look at the specific promotability behaviors that supported these women's advancement, including what they were told by their managers they were doing well—insights that positioned them for promotion. These reflections illustrate through their own narratives on what boosted their confidence.

Renell shared what their current CIO stated in an open forum when asked about his recommendation for those seeking promotions: "If you are looking for a promotion, you want to set up a time and just start getting to know those decision-makers a little better. Most anyone I know would be open if you put a thirty-minute thing on their calendar. It does not matter how high up in the organization they are." She agreed with this advice, stating that decision-makers behave more favorably toward those they already know through experience than toward someone with excellent experience they cannot relate to.

Cynthia, who also worked for a non-profit healthcare organization, said they value relationships and how well the staff relates to their supervisor. She has two master's degrees and believed "the more education I have, the more opportunities I will get. But it is not necessarily true. It is about people's experience and ability to do the job." From her perspective, experience and competence are essential in addition to familiarity and relationship with the manager.

Jing also attested that their company values all the index items but that sometimes individuals with stronger social networks were more likely to gain promotional positions than those without them. She stated, "Some people just have stronger relationships with some of the leadership that maybe were nurtured a certain way to move into some of those positions."

Sue shared the importance of networking and the ability to take on roles and responsibilities of a promotion based on both the qualitative and quantitative metrics of existing projects. She reported that experience and skills matter, but the managers' opinions, the size of one's professional network, and the number of people one has worked with also affect promotability. "If your manager is not as engaged with you," she said, "or might not understand the role, you might see a variance in an individual's career, path, or projection."

Serena reported that their company values academic prestige, hires people from Ivy League colleges and top companies, and then continues to promote them. These are identified as "best people" or "top talent." When specifically asked about social networking or relationship building, she said, "None of that is valued. It is how you present your critical thinking." According to her:

> The company was under-indexed in terms of social capital and emotional intelligence during the COVID-19 pandemic. People from a privileged background with an elite education and elite companies have not experienced the turmoil and challenges in life. Whereas, for minority communities and women, the world has always been challenging, and they have developed skills to function and have naturally developed resilience. These differences have become more obvious in the last three years and cannot be measured. These are not part of the values that are stated. These are not part of the evaluation or interview process or reward system. But now, after the COVID-19 pandemic, these are starting to surface, and a lot of programming or education series provided by the company to the employees is around these elements.

Thus, she highlights marginalized groups' challenges and urges companies to pay attention to skills developed by minorities in the face of adversity.

Diva mentioned that as part of the pharmaceutical industry, their company had traditionally valued education and experience (or business knowledge). She reported a recent shift in the company's emphasis on a collaborative environment, focusing on reducing redundancies in the processes and retaining projects that bring value. She characterized self-promotion as being a spokesperson of oneself, speaking up or advocating for oneself, and showcasing or promoting work accomplishments to leadership.

In addition to the examples identified in the question, she spoke about the value of taking additional stretch assignments, sharing knowledge with cross-functional teams, and volunteering or giving back to the community. She indicated the benefits by stating, "When you take additional stretch assignments and are ready to expand more and help others, that has impacted me, or has been a positive addition, a star on my career." She also mentioned connecting with old managers and conducting knowledge sharing sessions related to new technical success and her team's success.

Sheniqua, who worked as a community organizer in a non-profit company, said that the organization values community (or customers) and wants to make sure the community has the necessary resources. She also mentioned that the company values the customer and the financial bottom line when making promotion decisions. She said, "Performance is valued, but people in sales who bring more money get promoted. They will get the biggest bonuses. They will have the most visibility. They will get the most recognition." As director of talent management, she has been advocating for senior leaders to focus on learning and growth for employees. She acknowledged that the company is trying hard to be more vigilant about how it recognizes people and has started employee recognition programs.

Naomi mentioned that individuals, including herself, have recently been identified based on their demographics and nominated for promotion to meet the quota for promoting diverse individuals. She said the company values emotional intelligence, agility, and a commercial mindset. According to her, managing and meeting people at different levels requires emotional intelligence. She believes that managers need to be able to step back, listen, and assess the situation before making decisions.

Promotion practices today are not created in a vacuum; they are shaped by decades, if not centuries, of systemic exclusion. To fully grasp the inequities present in modern workplaces, we must first understand their historical context. From discriminatory policies to cultural norms that excluded women and minorities, these historical systems have left a legacy. The next chapter traces the roots of these inequities, showing how the past continues to influence the present. The chapter also highlights how trust in the system and personnel plays a pivotal role in retention.

8
THE TRUST BEHIND
THE TITLE

IN EVERY CAREER journey, the pathway to promotion is rarely defined by talent alone. While skills and performance matter, what often sets someone apart is the foundation of trust built between the employee and the manager. Trust is not a vague or optional element; it is a decisive factor that influences who gets considered for greater responsibility.

At its core, a promotion is not simply a reward; it is a risk taken by a manager. It signals that they believe you are ready to carry forward the mission of the team or organization. For that decision to happen, the manager must feel confident not just in what you do, but in how you do it—your judgment, reliability, alignment with values, and your ability to navigate complexity without losing sight of the bigger picture. The next two chapters explore how trust is built, how it is tested, and why it remains a crucial, often unspoken, driver for promoting truthlighting. Through the voices and stories of women who have earned or been denied promotions, we unpack the invisible yet powerful dynamics that shape careers. Because behind every promotion is a vote of confidence—and that vote begins with trust.

Trust typically involves dependency on the actions of another party. A relationship between manager and employee is solid with a firm belief in the competence of an entity to act dependably, securely, and reliably within a specified context.[83] Employers may be more likely to promote someone if they have confidence in their abilities, knowledge, and skills. Likewise, an employee is far more likely to accept their vulnerability if they have positive expectations of the intentions or actions of the employer.

An assessment of such trustworthiness in the employee-employer relationship often determines the confidence level of the trusted party.[47] The most utilized model of interpersonal trustworthiness includes three components:

1. Ability: Perceived skills and competence of the trusted party

2. Benevolence: The extent to which the trusted party is believed to want to do good to the trusting party

3. Integrity: Perception that the trusted party will act under a set of principles and values that the trusting party finds acceptable[84]

Although little is known about managers' perception and trustworthiness of employees' abilities and the intentions and integrity in making promotions and rewards decisions, research shows that trust in both the system and the manager is essential for the full impact and effectiveness of the performance appraisal system. Performance appraisal systems cannot be examined in isolation; they must be understood within the context of their given function and the organization's needs. The nature of trust in the system rather than interpersonal trust, including organizational characteristics, such as values, principles, and standards of behaviors that have been internalized, has a significant role in the appraisal context.[47] Future research requires exploration of the effects of relationship elements, such as trust in human resource (HR) practices around promotion.[63]

This trust in the system and a relational exchange, rather than a purely economic exchange, enables the employee commitment and performance needed for organizational survival and prosperity.[47] Those who perceive the allocation of promotion (distributive justice) as unfair are the ones who question the process of promotion decision-making (procedural justice) compared to those who perceive it as fair.[55] Trust may matter more as a predictor of outcomes when perceptions of distributive justice are low rather than high.[85] Hence, trust becomes a principal factor when making conclusions about one's attitudes, behaviors, and reactions to the system. If the individual views the system as trustworthy, this will counteract the potential negative impacts of low distributive justice.[47]

Internal employees who do not receive a promotion or raise remain dissatisfied, impacting the organization's future development.[86] Moreover, those who report higher organizational commitment are more affected by the perceived unfairness of layoff decisions than those who report low organizational commitment.[47] Hence, identification with and commitment to the employer strongly influences how people react to decisions made by the employer.

The conversation of potential career development begins with the performance appraisal process. The appraisal process demonstrates the intentions and behaviors of both employees and managers. Managers typically control, monitor, and assess employee behaviors to determine annual raises, bonuses, or rewards, termed an economic exchange.[87] Trust creates and is created by a positive social exchange relationship, where parties choose to provide benefit to the other and have confidence they will not feel exploited or taken advantage of.[47,88] Positive perception of the performance appraisal process is associated with greater employee trust in their managers and the organization.[89]

Trust encourages open communication and builds confidence in what two or more individuals can achieve by working together. Companies that are not concerned about the well-being of their employees and focus only on material gains and the organization's bottom line cannot effectively exercise kindness and trust. At the same time, companies that want to retain their positive self-image and brand need to build trust with customers and think about financial gains. "Kindness and trust are key ingredients of any worthy relationship."[90] Hence, balancing customers' and employees' needs is vital.

Trust helps employees build confidence in each other and aids in the team's ability to perform the tasks effectively. Trust helps increase open communication and effective problem-solving among teams. Employees go beyond their job requirements if they can openly communicate their challenges. If leaders favor certain employees over others, it jeopardizes the trust among employees and trust in management. On the contrary, if employees trust mid-level managers, there is increased cooperation and a heightened employee perception of fairness.[90]

Leaders need to care about their employees' professional development to win their employees' trust. Leaders must also value and recognize every team member's strengths and unique contributions and reward them accordingly. Leaders need to provide an environment where diverse subgroups can appreciate their differences and celebrate their similarities. As the number of diverse subgroups increases within an organization, it predisposes the subgroups to unequal and unfair treatment from the majority group. Hence, inclusion practices are essential for equitable treatment of all subgroups and building trust in the system.

The narratives shared by these women highlight a recurring theme: the pervasive impact of bias in workplace practices. From hiring decisions to promotions, these biases often operate subtly, but their effects are anything but small. These biases must be identified, addressed, and mitigated to create inclusive workplaces. The following chapter explores the critical steps managers can take to reduce bias and create environments where everyone has an equal opportunity to succeed.

Relationship with Manager

In this section I want to highlight the importance of trust in a good working relationship as a key ingredient for receiving a promotion.

It includes the patterns and themes that emerged in response to interview question, "How does the leader-follower relationship impact the promotion decision-making?" It also summarizes their perceptions, which provide insight into the manager's role in their promotion experience, the nature of the manager's relationship with them, and how it impacted the specific promotion outcome. The elements of the relationship are grouped in Table 7 below as women directly speak to the ingredients of a trusting relationship. These ingredients correlate with the positive experiences of those who received promotions. These elements speak to a transactional relationship between a leader and a follower, referenced by nine of the women as a good working relationship, seven as an open and transparent exchange of ideas, four as a relationship of trust, three as giving and receiving feedback, and three as interpersonal connection as illustrated in Table

115

7. Based on the women's report, this trusting relationship has enhanced managers' confidence in employees' ability to meet expectations by reciprocating through favorable behavior. The narratives from the interviews support the existing literature on trust and promotion in Chapter 8, where trust is an essential condition of social exchange. Better interpersonal relationships facilitate trust building and favorable behaviors between the trusted parties for the benefit of the other.[86] As shown in Table 7, the interpersonal connection was described by women as having a casual relationship without formalities where they could laugh with their managers and have a rapport that feels safe to share their ideas. Giving and receiving feedback (reported by four of the women) and open, transparent communication (reported by seven women) are the key ingredients for building trust.

Manager Behaviors that Perpetuate Gaslighting

Lack of self-awareness, making assumptions, rigidity, lack of honesty in communication, and lack of understanding of advanced careers and how to provide a path for growth were some of the behaviors that negatively impacted the relationship with the manager and the promotion outcome. In the narrative, you will see how these behaviors can perpetuate gaslighting by creating confusion, eroding trust, and causing employees to question their own perceptions, capabilities, and career readiness.

Renell reported revealing too much about her background to her team and hiring manager. This worked to her disadvantage because the hiring manager made assumptions about her. However, her relationship with her manager's manager got her the promotion. Chanell felt it was a burden to do self-advocacy and shared her frustration about not receiving validation for her ideas and hard work. She would have liked her manager to say, "I am confident you will do this, and I believe in you." She felt the manager did not understand her role or how she could grow. The manager understood her role based solely on what other managers said she was doing. She felt there was a lack of honesty in the relationship. She expected her manager to have had the necessary conversations with industry experts to gain further insight into her role and to give her feedback and advice.

Cynthia also confessed from her experience as a manager that boundaries are often blurred when promotions are relationship-based and when there is a sense of connection that may feel too personal. She was self-aware and shared an example of being friends with one of her employees. When a promotion opportunity became available, she was biased and wanted her friend to get the position, and she advocated for her friend versus other candidates.

Relationship that Promotes Truthlighting

The following narratives illustrate the dynamics of manager-employee communication that exemplify truthlighting, highlighting stories of women whose managers communicated in ways that reinforced their confidence and sense of value.

Sheniqua characterized a good working relationship as an open and transparent relationship in which they can talk about anything with their manager, especially about family. Cynthia felt that those with a rapport with their manager have more opportunities for promotion, and getting along with people is vital because it facilitates teamwork. Rita said she has open and honest conversations and discussions with her manager, who does not micromanage her and trusts her to get things done. Maya reported that she has quarterly check-ins with her manager to give and receive constructive feedback on things she can do differently. She reported receiving positive feedback that she was doing well and meeting all expectations. She further noted that it makes her feel empowered to go to someone with problems, someone who trusts her and has her back. Maya also shared having an easy, transparent relationship and having worked to build trust. Naomi said she has a good working relationship with her manager, who calls her to get her opinion when something happens. She reported that they trust each other, which is essential in the retail industry. Renell said she has a "straight shooter" relationship in which her manager would not hold back in providing feedback, and the team can comfortably articulate when they need to change directions. Renell also recognized that while a good relationship of trust requires openness, one needs to be wary of what to share and what not to share. Diva reported having yearly conversations with her manager about her five-year goals. She attested that she could obtain feedback and advice from the manager when she went off-course, which helped her understand stakeholders' expectations. She said her manager communicated her expectations and ensured the new position was a good fit for her.

Table 7

Factors of Leader-Member Exchange Relationship

Leader-Member Exchange	References to Words	Number of Participants	Number of References
Relationship with Manager	Good Working Relationship	9	11
	Open and Transparent	7	10
	Trust	6	7
	Feedback	4	6
	Interpersonal Connection	3	3
	Rapport	2	3
	Casual	2	2
	Shared Value/Vision	1	1
	Feel Safe	1	1
	Frustration and No Validation	1	1
	No Formalities	1	1
	Laugh	1	1
Manager Behaviors	Supportive	7	9
	Root for Employee	6	9
	Provide Growth Opportunity	5	8
	Advocate	4	6
	Confident in Employee	3	6
	Encourage/Empower	2	3
	Provide Voice	2	2
	Provide Visibility	2	2
	Role Model	1	1
	Rigid	1	1
	Educate Themselves	1	1

Role of Manager

In this section, I summarize key takeaways and behaviors that foster truthlighting. The following manager behaviors, identified through interviews, contribute to enhancing employee confidence and increasing their promotability:

1. Be an advocate

2. Provide growth opportunities

3. Be supportive of employee goals and interests

▶ Advocate

This section includes quotes and references about a manager's role as an advocate from the women I interviewed.

According to the *Merriam-Webster* (n.d.) dictionary, an advocate defends or maintains a cause or proposal, supports or promotes the interest of a cause or a group, and pleads for the cause of another. The women's perceptions indicate that when managers advocate for their employees and promote the best interests of their employees, it yields a positive promotion outcome. In addition, the women reported that their manager provided growth opportunities in the form of visibility and voice.

Sue attributed her success to the company's process of providing her with an advisor and a career path in addition to putting in hard work and aligning herself with "really good supportive advocates." She has been promoted twice in six years in a large consulting firm, which is rare. She attributes this success to a full package of company values, supportive mentors and managers, and hard work that allowed her to build a strong and trusting group dynamic.

Maya had a transparent manager who worked in the background to get all team members what they deserved.

He told her, "If you're performing well and delivering all the things that you're expected to deliver, and you're meeting your goals, I will do everything I can to get you what you deserve."

Naomi emphasized the importance of an advocate to get noticed, especially in large companies where you don't typically get a chance to speak up. Her manager advocated for her when they had conversations related to talent and skills. The manager allowed her to lead in meetings so the leaders could hear her voice, opinion, and point of view and remember her. According to her, the manager allows her to have face time with people that most individuals in the company never have an opportunity to meet, let alone have a meeting with.

While most women felt they had the support of their managers, Chanell, who had a unique role and no defined career progression path, said she had to advocate for herself. She expressed, "I don't have a lot of people who look like me and are in power to help me feel more comfortable to advocate," which made it difficult for her to advocate for herself. From her perspective, advocacy is when you have direct access to a career advisor and can access information that others in the company cannot.

Six women described their managers as someone rooting for them. Rita said promotions are not based on skills or performance matrices in senior leadership roles. She said, "At her level, she needs a mentor or a sponsor who is going to bat for her and do something relatively fast when they know I am going to leave." Sue communicated her goals, and the manager said, "Yes, we can get you there."

❭ Provides Growth Opportunities

This section includes five quotes from the women who describe their manager as someone who provides growth opportunities in terms of giving visibility and voice.

Jaya reports that promotability depends on the hiring manager and whether they can influence the decision-makers and speak for the candidate because the manager is most familiar with the candidates' accomplishments. Sue said, "My manager, mentor, and advocate is a middle-aged White male who's been in the industry for many years. He brought me in to support on strategy, although I was new, and that meant the opportunity to sit at a table alongside our leaders." He told her, "I want you to have a voice at the table." Maya's manager told her, "You are in my succession plan. I will expose you to more stuff. I want to groom you for the next step." Jing reported that her manager intentionally tried to find ways to position her within the department to get peripheral experience, position her for high-profile projects, and get her in front of leadership. Naomi reported that her managers allowed her to have a face-to-face presence with leaders most people never have the chance to meet. Her manager allowed her to lead.

▶ Create a Safe Environment

Many of the women who received a promotion attribute it to support from their manager. Supportive managers provide a safe environment for employees to speak up and thrive. Managers who allowed them to promote the behaviors that the company values were considered supportive. Seven women said that their managers were supportive of their goals. This support is demonstrated as providing flexibility such as personal time off when needed (reported Sheniqua), being fair and providing equal opportunity to everyone (reported Cynthia), not micromanaging (reported Rita), sharing expectations and information (reported Diva), and providing encouragement (reported Cynthia, Jaya, Sue, and Jing). As per Renell, managers who are confident in their employees' abilities know they can do the work, and they want them in the role. In her interview, her manager told her she would do a great job.

My findings validate research on social connectedness or the extent of cultural and social similarity between managers and employees, leading to effective LMX.[70] Six women attested that similarity in race, age, or gender attributed to success in the promotion outcome or increase in one's promotability rating. Chanell alluded to affinity bias as a factor that impacts the promotion outcome; that is, those in the affinity circle receive promotions quicker than those who are not. Maya wondered whether her manager's race being like hers affected her promotion. Naomi referenced that her manager was about her age, which facilitated a good working relationship. Maya mentioned having phenomenal managers is a key factor— whether male or female. However, she reported feeling that such support is more typical with female managers because they tend to watch out for other women and take them under their wings. They say, "We have to watch out for each other."

Bias is a complex and deeply ingrained issue, but it is not insurmountable. Through intentional action and structured approaches, organizations can begin to reduce their influence and promote equity. This requires understanding the problem and implementing practical solutions that drive measurable change. The next chapter introduces an action-oriented framework, providing tools and strategies to guide organizations toward fairness and inclusion.

9
AN ACTION-ORIENTED FRAMEWORK

THIS BOOK SERVES to educate workplace leadership about the challenges faced by minority women in mid-level management as they relate to merit evaluation, salary growth, and promotions. It also calls attention to the benefits of providing a supportive environment for growth and resources for professional development and career advancement based on the women's responses to all survey questions—specifically, to the question, "What, in your opinion, needs to be done differently to address subjective bias from the promotion decision-making process?"

I have created an action-oriented framework for HR, managers, and employees to reduce bias in the workplace. Figure 2 illustrates my framework, and in the remainder of this chapter, I will explain how to apply the framework in any workplace.

Thirteen of the women reported that they experience subjective bias in the workplace, and most believed this bias cannot be eliminated because it is unconscious. By standardizing the promotion process and reducing subjective bias through implicit bias training and self-awareness, the promotion process may become fairer and more equitable than it currently is.

I have developed a compendium of promotability behaviors that provide actionable steps for employees to increase their promotability rating. Managers can imitate the manager behaviors identified in this book. Both employees and managers can practice behaviors that enhance the quality of their relationship. The career advancement opportunities and programs narrated by the women (summarized in Chapter 2) can be modeled by companies and customized based on the DEI priorities and needs.

Figure 2

Framework to Reduce Bias in the Promotion Process and Increase Promotability

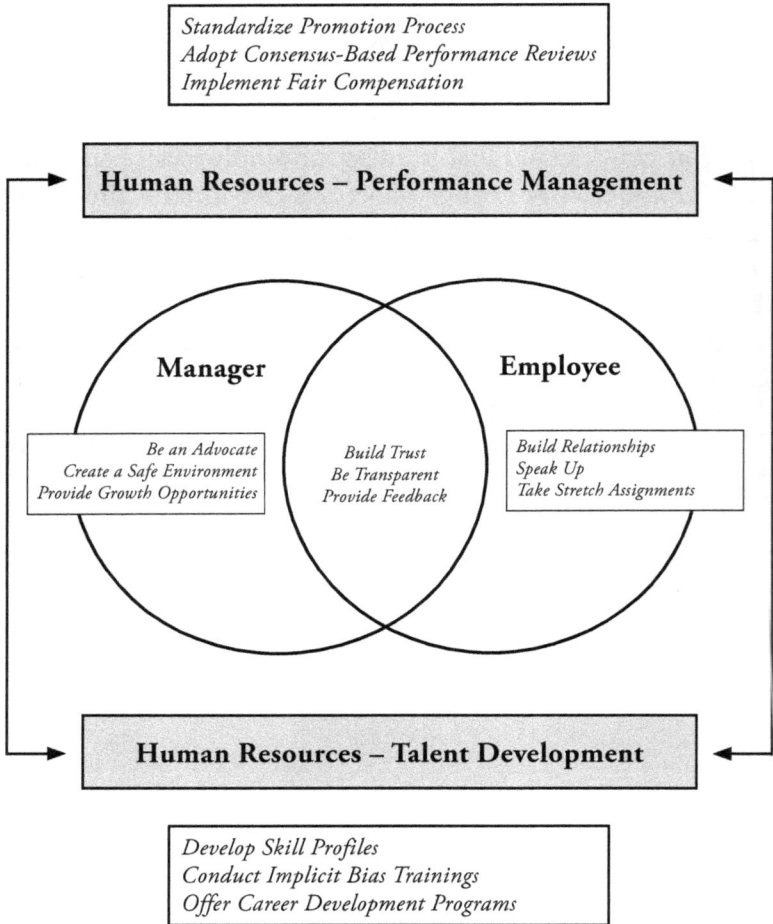

Standardize Promotion Process
Adopt Consensus-Based Performance Reviews
Implement Fair Compensation

Human Resources – Performance Management

Manager

Employee

Be an Advocate
Create a Safe Environment
Provide Growth Opportunities

Build Trust
Be Transparent
Provide Feedback

Build Relationships
Speak Up
Take Stretch Assignments

Human Resources – Talent Development

Develop Skill Profiles
Conduct Implicit Bias Trainings
Offer Career Development Programs

This framework is designed to depict specific actions for HR, managers, and employees. The overlapping area of the circles in Figure 2 indicates various qualities of the leader-follower relationship. HR actions are divided into two key functions: performance management and talent development. It will reduce bias as HR teams work cohesively toward the identified actions. The managers' behaviors, employees' behaviors, and relationships together increase promotability. The following sections explain the framework in detail.

HR Performance Management Actions

I recognize the critical role that human resources and performance management systems play in ensuring fairness and transparency in promotions by standardizing processes such as job postings, announcement protocols, and structured decision-making.

To standardize the promotion process, HR can focus on standardizing the application process by universally posting open positions for the entire company and providing equal opportunity to individuals throughout the company rather than only informing those individuals within an immediate team or a manager's circle of familiarity (reported by Cynthia).

The position descriptions can be transparent to include the specific team the position is posted for, the immediate hiring manager, and the salary grade level or compensation. Chanell recommended that companies include more insight into the role that is opening and what is required for the position in the job requisition. The announcements for promotion opportunities can be made regularly via email or company portals. HR managers can recommend a diverse slate of applicants whose skills, qualifications, and performance match the position's requirements.

This selection process can be closely monitored to prevent subjective bias and can incorporate recommendations of eligible candidates from managers within different departments. Organizations can utilize a talent management system, including a repository of employee skills and abilities under their employee profile. These skills and abilities can be transferable across positions and visible to hiring managers (reported by Tara and Maya) across the organization.

The promotion decision-making process needs to be examined to reduce subjective bias by implementing a diverse interview panel, including leaders and managers from different departments, who can vote for the final candidate, question any affinity bias or factors that may render the process unfair, and obtain feedback from the applicant's immediate manager about their accomplishments. The performance evaluation process needs to be prioritized as a focus area to adopt consensus-based performance reviews. A team of managers reviews the individual's performance, obtains 360-degree feedback across other disciplines, and comes to a consensus on the individual's performance rating.

To tackle the issues of frequent leadership turnover, performance reviews can include clear documentation of an individual's accomplishments that can be referenced when the position becomes available (as per Tara) and develop career development goals that new managers can reference. Cynthia recommended that companies develop a way to archive and share employee accomplishments with everyone on the company portal. Rigid HR policies and practices, such as a promotion or raise cap, diversity quota, and tenure requirements, need to be examined with a DEI lens to ensure there is equity in pay and fair compensation comparable to the job duties and responsibilities of the position at a given point in time. Several assessment tools are available to identify individuals with leadership/management skills and can be used to reduce subjective bias in the selection process.

HR Talent Development: Fostering a Culture of Equity

Based on the themes emerging from the interviews, implicit bias and self-awareness training are critical tools for helping individuals reflect on their assumptions, reduce unintentional harm, and contribute to a more inclusive and equitable workplace.

Organizations can mandate implicit bias training and other training to increase self-awareness and reduce subjective bias among decision-makers. Implicit bias training helps with self-awareness, checking one's biases, speaking up when something is wrong, and learning how to facilitate a real change (reported by Rita, Sima, and Jing). Rita recommended bringing people who have taken career breaks to raise their children back into the workforce and encouraging job sharing between retirees. This will address bias related to critical events that put individuals out of the workforce.

Intentional employee socialization experiences are essential for fostering a sense of belonging, aligning individuals with organizational values, and supporting long-term engagement. Employee socialization experiences can focus on inclusion and belongingness to encourage minority participation and opportunity for face-to-face time with skip-level management and senior leaders (reported Sima). Sima also recommended providing more glamor and visibility to women by allowing them the opportunity to present at major technology conferences. Serena, who is leading a Black community group, shared that when they started their discussions among underrepresented groups, they realized that their individual experiences were collective experiences and that they were victims of microaggression in the disguise of constructive feedback. These microaggressions included suggestions that they bring in vendors to provide professional development programs for Black employees and the implication that Black members of the organization need more coaching than their peers. This reinforced the belief that a deficit in the community prevents Black members of the company from being a representative population of the company and that they "just aren't good enough."

Serena said, "When something is not fair, it is the least fair for the most oppressed among us." She implemented a two-pronged approach of educating managers to understand the nature of these microaggressions and then holding managers accountable for developing the skill sets needed to manage and understand the nuances of managing diverse teams as a mentor. Serena and Jing further expressed that their companies had gaps in perspective and skill sets because of a lack of representation of minority populations across leadership initiatives. Sue recommended bringing in speakers to train individuals on how to be a professional who continues to progress and get promoted and how to navigate the challenges of being a mother in the workforce.

It is also recommended to measure the impact of such trainings and activities to reduce bias in selection/recruitment interviewing and presenting diverse slates. This includes measuring internally how many are on a professional development plan (diverse slate) and how many are considered and granted promotion. Stay away from the vertical hierarchy and create a more horizontal hierarchy.

Employee's Role: Promote Yourself and Speak Up

In my view, employees play a vital role in their own growth by taking initiative to align their development with both personal and organizational goals.

Promotability behaviors are actionable behaviors that allow for visibility and self-promotion to create an impression on decision-makers and increase promotability ratings. Networking and relationship-building were rated highest among the women for a successful promotion outcome. They frequently shared promotability behaviors, including taking stretch assignments, speaking up, and having a learning attitude. Table 6 highlights other promotability behaviors that demonstrate employee readiness for promotion. Diva mentioned the importance of self-promotion, engaging in activities to get noticed, and taking stretch assignments.

Most women I interviewed reported that they worked harder than their peers and had to prove they were worthy of their promotion to get fair compensation and an equivalent rank. Sima shared the importance of collaborating with leaders from other departments and volunteering as behavior that created a positive impression. My research revealed that individuals who are articulate, camera-ready, present a good face to the public, and can represent the company well have higher promotability ratings in companies that are customer focused.

Manager's Role: From Othering to Understanding

To move from othering to understanding, managers must first recognize their own biases and actively seek to learn about the lived experiences, values, and perspectives of those who are different from them. I see that this shift requires deep listening, asking respectful questions, and creating space for authentic voices to be heard without judgment. Managers can foster inclusion by building relationships rooted in empathy, curiosity, and shared goals—transforming difference from a barrier into a bridge.

The women who received promotions attributed their success to the support of their managers. Managers need to advocate for their employees to senior leadership and provide opportunities that provide them with exposure and a voice at the table. Managers play a key role in creating a safe environment for everyone to give and receive open feedback. Table 7 outlines the manager behaviors the women found beneficial to the positive promotion outcome. Managers can engage in periodic self-assessments to check their biases and seek training to increase self-awareness.

Tara said that the managers should know everyone on the team, their background, the top performers, and their goals and career aspirations. When there are leadership changes, managers should understand the talent pool they are working with and what their team members have accomplished. Five of the women who received promotions suggested that managers should make a business case, remain proactive in developing individuals for their next potential roles, and help them define their career paths.

Throughout the book, firsthand stories from women reveal a persistent pressure to prove themselves, often leading to self-doubt. Supportive managers who provide regular feedback and frequent validation can play a crucial role in alleviating these feelings and fostering confidence. I have gleaned four important takeaways from the stories of these women. They require intentional mentoring, frequent validation, active feedback, and encouragement to achieve their highest potential, as they are navigating systems in which they are not adequately represented and may face obstacles.

Shared Actions for Managers and Employees: Bridging the Gap

Effective performance management is rooted in mutual accountability and open communication. When managers and employees commit to a shared development process, they create an environment where feedback is not only expected but valued. I want to emphasize the significance of a collaborative approach that reinforces clarity, strengthens alignment on goals, and supports both individual and team success.

Remaining open and transparent allows managers to foster good working relationships with frequent exchanges of ideas. A culture of real-time bidirectional feedback facilitates trust, and trust-building and problem-solving ultimately increase managers' confidence in employees' abilities to deal with high-stakes situations. The ingredients of a high-quality LMX relationship are shown in Table 7.

Equity in promotions is achievable, but it requires commitment, accountability, and courage to challenge existing systems. The frameworks and strategies discussed in this book provide a starting point for meaningful change. As we conclude, we'll revisit the key takeaways and outline clear next steps for individuals and organizations. Together, we can create diverse and equitable workplaces.

ROADMAP FOR TRUTHLIGHTING: KEY TAKEAWAYS

AS WE REACH the end of this journey, one truth remains clear: The workplace is at its best when fairness, transparency, and integrity guide decision-making. We began by exposing the harmful effects of gaslighting—how it distorts reality, erodes trust, and creates barriers to equitable promotions. But we didn't stop there. Through the concept of truthlighting, we have redefined what a just and thriving workplace looks like—one where employees are valued for their contributions, where reality is affirmed rather than manipulated, and where career growth is based on merit, not manipulation. The path forward isn't just about eliminating gaslighting; it's about actively cultivating truthlighting behaviors that build trust, empower individuals, and ensure fair promotions become the norm, not the exception.

Embracing truthlighting in career advancement means actively challenging distortions, affirming one's value, and advocating for opportunities based on merit rather than perception. Employees who practice truthlighting reject self-doubt caused by bias or manipulation and instead take ownership of their growth by demonstrating their skills, contributions, and leadership potential.

Practice Promotability Behaviors

Demonstrating promotability behaviors increases an individual's chances of advancing within an organization. Companies evaluate a promotability index based on elements employees perceive as influencing promotions, while employees enhance their promotability by actively improving their performance, gaining relevant experience, deepening their knowledge, and meeting necessary qualifications. Building relationships and engaging in strategic self-promotion create visibility with senior leadership, further strengthening promotability ratings. Employees can enhance their readiness for higher-level responsibilities by:

1. **Taking on stretch assignments** to demonstrate capability beyond current job responsibilities

2. **Maintaining a learning mindset** to develop skills and adapt to new challenges continuously

3. **Speaking up in meetings** to showcase expertise, contribute ideas, and increase visibility

By incorporating truthlighting into their professional approach, employees can confidently navigate workplace challenges, ensuring their career growth is guided by their actual contributions rather than external biases or misrepresentations.

Truthlighting is crucial in shaping workplace relationships, ensuring trust is built on authenticity rather than subjective perceptions or hidden biases. Employees who embrace truthlighting communicate openly, advocate for themselves, and challenge inconsistencies in promotion practices. They create stronger, trust-based relationships with managers and leadership by affirming their contributions and fostering transparency. In an environment where truthlighting is practiced, employees and managers work toward equitable opportunities, reducing the impact of favoritism, social biases, or unclear advancement criteria.

Fostering a strong working relationship with managers builds trust and increases promotion opportunities. While many employees report experiencing unfair treatment, inconsistencies in the promotion application process and a lack of transparency in decision-making create uncertainty. Navigating frequent organizational changes and rigid policies presents additional challenges, while perceptions of inequities in pay and advancement often stem from factors like age, gender, race, and tenure. Experiencing bias—whether through social and cultural similarities with managers or other subjective influences—affects promotion outcomes. Employees can strengthen trust with leadership and improve their promotability by:

1. **Building trust with managers** to enhance leader-member exchange (LMX) and demonstrate reliability

2. **Strengthening social connections** within the workplace to foster professional visibility

By incorporating truthlighting into their approach, employees can cultivate relationships built on fairness and merit, ensuring their career growth is determined by their contributions rather than external biases.

Managers play a crucial role in shaping employees' perceptions of fairness and influencing positive promotion outcomes. Employees, particularly those from underrepresented groups, benefit from managers who actively support their career growth through mentorship, feedback, and advocacy. Ensuring all employees have equal access to development opportunities fosters a workplace culture where promotions are based on merit rather than subjective biases. Managers can strengthen employee promotability by:

1. **Providing proactive mentorship** to guide employees in career planning and skill development

2. **Offering frequent validation** to recognize contributions and reinforce employees' value within the organization

3. **Delivering regular feedback** to help employees refine their skills and align with promotion expectations

4. **Encouraging self-promotion** by supporting employees in showcasing their achievements and leadership potential

5. **Facilitating relationship-building** by creating networking opportunities and ensuring employees gain visibility with decision-makers

By actively engaging in these behaviors, managers enhance employees' promotability and contribute to a more equitable and transparent promotion process within the organization. True workplace equity isn't just about removing obstacles; it's about intentionally creating systems that uplift and support all employees in their career journeys.

However, the responsibility of fostering fairness and transparency doesn't rest on managers alone. Organizations must implement systemic changes that reinforce truthlighting at every level—embedding equity, accountability, and structural safeguards into promotion practices. The following frameworks outline key organizational strategies to ensure that fair and merit-based career advancement becomes the standard, not the exception.

Promote Systemic Change

Creating a workplace where truthlighting thrives requires more than individual actions; it demands systemic change at the organizational level. While employees and managers play a role in fostering fairness and transparency, organizations must take deliberate steps to embed truthlighting into their policies, structures, and leadership practices. This means designing systems that ensure equitable access to career advancement, mitigate bias in decision-making, and cultivate an environment where all employees are empowered to succeed based on their contributions and potential. Organizations can move beyond surface-level diversity efforts and create lasting, structural equity by implementing comprehensive frameworks for fair opportunity, career advancement, and empowerment. The following frameworks and tools (see Appendix C) provide actionable strategies to promote truthlighting, ensuring that fairness, inclusion, and transparency become fundamental aspects of workplace culture.

❭ Provide Fair Opportunity

Truthlighting for fair opportunities involves exposing the hidden barriers and systemic inequalities that may prevent certain groups of employees from accessing equal opportunities. It requires leaders to acknowledge disparities in career advancement, compensation, and access to resources while creating a transparent environment where these issues can be openly discussed and addressed. By shining a light on these challenges, organizations can intentionally create a level playing field where every employee has a fair chance to succeed.

All employees, regardless of gender, race, background, or personal connections, should have an equal chance to advance based on their skills, experience, and performance. Promotions should be transparent, merit-based, and free from biases that favor certain groups disproportionately. A fair promotion opportunity means that every employee has an equal chance to advance based on their qualifications, contributions, and potential rather than factors like personal biases, favoritism, or systemic barriers. Promotions are often influenced by subjective opinions, informal networks, or unstructured decision-making, which can disadvantage certain groups, particularly women, minorities, and those without strong executive sponsors.

When employees believe they have a legitimate shot at career growth, they are more engaged, motivated, and committed to their work. This sense of fairness enhances individual morale and strengthens an organization's culture by fostering trust and reducing turnover. However, achieving true fairness requires organizations to move beyond good intentions and build structured, transparent promotion frameworks that minimize bias and ensure all employees can compete on a level playing field. Organizations can use the Fair-Opportunity Framework in Appendix C to create an environment where promotions are earned fairly, and every employee has a real opportunity to succeed. This framework outlines practical strategies for ensuring that opportunities for growth, recognition, and promotion are equitable for all employees.

▶ Develop Inclusive Leadership Competencies

Truthlighting in inclusive leadership is the practice of bringing difficult realities to light within an organization, such as hidden biases, systemic inequities, and disparities in opportunities. It involves leaders openly confronting these uncomfortable truths and creating a culture where employees feel safe and empowered to discuss diversity, equity, and inclusion issues. This transparent approach fosters accountability and drives real change, helping to create a more equitable environment for all.

Elements from the Promotability Index can be used to create assessment tools for minority women to evaluate their promotability, ensuring that these tools are both culturally sensitive and validated for diverse populations. While many leadership assessment tools are available, few are tailored to the unique challenges underrepresented groups face. Appendix C includes a framework for developing inclusive leadership skills and empowering leaders to foster growth and opportunity for all. This framework provides actionable steps for leaders to adopt inclusive leadership practices, supporting the development of a diverse and inclusive workplace culture.

▶ Drive Career Advancement and Empowerment for All

Truthlighting for career advancement and empowerment involves shedding light on the barriers and biases that hinder employees, particularly those from underrepresented groups, from advancing in their careers. It encourages leaders to confront the uncomfortable truths about unequal access to growth opportunities, mentorship, and promotions while fostering a culture of transparency and accountability. By openly addressing these challenges, organizations empower employees to take control of their career paths and ensure all individuals, regardless of background, have the tools and support they need to succeed.

The women I interviewed are looking for support and advocacy from their managers to advance in their careers. Data supports the literature regarding male and White domination in senior leadership roles, resulting in the further perpetuation of the glass ceiling, stereotypes, and discrimination. There are different career advancement programs for minorities that the women have found to be effective, including training and professional development, mentorship or sponsorship, individual career plans, employee/business resource groups, recognition, and rewards. Appendix C includes a Career Advancement and Empowerment Framework that can be utilized to implement such programs. This framework offers strategies to create an environment where career advancement is truly accessible, fair, and empowering for everyone.

▶ Mitigate Bias and Promote Transparent Communication

Truthlighting in the context of bias mitigation and transparent communication involves shedding light on the hidden biases and inequities that may influence organizational decisions and actions. By actively confronting these issues, leaders can promote a culture of openness where biases are acknowledged and addressed, and communication is clear, honest, and consistent. This approach fosters accountability and trust, ensuring all employees have equal opportunities to succeed.

This book outlines the experiences of minority women in mid-level management seeking career advancement into senior leadership roles. The findings reveal inconsistent promotion opportunities and subjective biases in decision-making. While most of the women I interviewed identified bias, a significant number felt they were treated fairly, attributing this to positive relationships with their managers. Appendix C includes a Bias Mitigation and Transparent Communication Framework, Unconscious Bias Awareness Exercise, and Privilege Self-Reflection Tool for identifying personal biases and privileges, which can help foster greater transparency, accountability, and fairness in the promotion process. This framework provides actionable strategies for mitigating bias and promoting transparent communication, which is essential for creating a fair and inclusive workplace.

RESOURCES AND TOOLS

Fair Opportunity Framework for Workplace Promotions

Purpose: Guide HR and managers in evaluating promotion processes for fairness and consistency, ensuring all employees have equitable opportunities for advancement. This framework provides a structured approach to assessing, improving, and maintaining fairness in promotions.

1. Audit the Current Promotion Process

Understanding the existing promotion landscape is the first step in identifying areas for improvement and reducing systemic inequities.

Key Actions:

- Collect promotion rate data segmented by demographic factors, such as race, gender, tenure, and department.

- Conduct employee surveys to assess perceptions of fairness and inclusivity in the promotion process.

- Evaluate current promotion criteria, decision-making processes, and leadership involvement for consistency and transparency.

- Compare internal promotion rates with industry benchmarks to assess organizational progress.

- Review past promotion decisions to identify patterns of disparities or favoritism.

- Identify barriers that minority employees face in accessing leadership opportunities.

Example:

An HR team at a mid-sized tech company discovered that women of color were underrepresented in leadership roles. Surveys revealed a perception that promotions favored employees with close personal relationships with decision-makers. This insight prompted the company to reevaluate its processes and include a diverse panel of leaders/managers in interview and promotion decision-making processes.

2. Establish Transparent Criteria for Promotions

Clear, standardized criteria help employees understand promotion requirements and minimize opportunities for subjective decision-making.

Key Actions:

- Define standard promotion criteria based on measurable competencies, leadership skills, and performance metrics.

- Collaborate with diverse stakeholders to ensure promotion standards reflect different work styles and contributions.

- All job descriptions and career pathways must include specific skills, experience levels, and performance expectations needed for advancement.

- Develop a formal succession planning process that aligns with career progression pathways.

- Ensure promotion criteria are widely accessible through internal communication channels, such as HR portals, town halls, and leadership meetings.

Example:

A healthcare organization revised its promotion criteria to emphasize leadership potential and measurable achievements. They shared this information in company-wide emails and workshops, ensuring all employees understood the requirements.

3. Train Decision-Makers on Bias Awareness

Unconscious biases influence hiring and promotion decisions, often disadvantaging underrepresented employees. Training equips managers and HR professionals with the tools to make fair, data-driven evaluations.

Key Actions:

- Implement mandatory training sessions on identifying and mitigating bias in promotion decisions to recognize and minimize favoritism, affinity bias, and gender/racial bias.

- Use case studies and real-world scenarios to help managers practice applying objective criteria.

- Train managers on assessing employees fairly using objective performance indicators by developing structured evaluation checklists.

- Encourage self-audits for hiring managers to reflect on past promotion decisions and identify patterns of bias.

Example:

A multinational corporation introduced quarterly bias-awareness workshops for all managers. These sessions included case studies highlighting common biases and strategies to counteract them during evaluations.

4. Implement Structured Evaluation Processes

Standardizing promotion evaluations helps ensure fairness and consistency across departments.

Key Actions:

- Use blind evaluations where possible to remove identifying information and focus on objective qualifications.

- Multiple reviewers are required to assess promotion candidates independently before finalizing decisions.

- Document the rationale behind all promotion decisions to create accountability and transparency.

- Introduce calibration meetings where leaders align on promotion criteria and outcomes to reduce inconsistencies.

Example:

A non-profit organization implemented a structured evaluation process where a panel of reviewers assessed candidates using a detailed rubric. By documenting every decision, they reduced bias and increased transparency.

5. Monitor and Measure Outcomes

Regularly tracking promotion outcomes ensures the framework remains effective and responsive to organizational needs.

Key Actions:

- Analyze promotion rates and outcomes annually, segmented by demographic groups.

- Use employee feedback surveys to measure perceptions of fairness and inclusivity in career advancement opportunities.

- Adjust policies and practices based on data findings to address persistent inequities.

- Establish benchmarks for leadership diversity and track progress toward meeting equity.

Example:

A manufacturing firm conducted annual equity audits and shared the results with leadership. Over three years, they saw a 15 percent increase in minority representation in management roles and an improved perception of fairness on surveys.

6. Foster Open Communication and Feedback

Building a culture of trust and engagement requires continuous dialogue between employees and leadership.

Key Actions:

- Hold regular town halls, focus groups, and Q&A sessions to discuss promotion policies and address employee concerns.

- Provide constructive feedback to employees who apply for promotions, outlining areas for growth and future opportunities.

- Create anonymous channels for employees to report concerns or suggest improvements in promotion policies.

- Encourage senior leaders to openly discuss their commitment to equitable promotions and provide transparency on organizational goals.

Example:

A financial services company created an anonymous suggestion box where employees could provide feedback on the promotion process. This input led to significant improvements in their criteria and communication strategies.

▶ Final Thoughts

Organizations implementing the Fair Opportunity Framework can create promotion systems rooted in fairness, transparency, and accountability. By auditing current practices, training decision-makers, and fostering open communication, companies can build trust and empower employees from all backgrounds to succeed.

This framework is designed to be adaptable, allowing organizations to tailor its components to their specific workforce needs while maintaining a commitment to equitable career advancement. This framework is not a one-size-fits-all solution but a customizable roadmap that evolves with the organization's needs. It offers a way forward for businesses committed to fairness, accountability, and long-term success.

Bias Mitigation and Transparent Communication Framework

Purpose: Reduce bias in decision-making processes, including hiring and promotions, while fostering open communication between employees and leadership to build trust and ensure transparency in equity and inclusion efforts. This framework provides structured steps to minimize bias and create a culture of openness and accountability.

1. Identify and Address Bias in Decision-Making

Organizations must first recognize where bias exists in their processes before they can take steps to eliminate it.

Key Actions:

- Conduct regular audits of hiring, promotions, and performance evaluations to identify disparities.

- Provide mandatory bias awareness training for managers and decision-makers, covering topics such as affinity bias, confirmation bias, and the halo effect.

- Use structured rubrics for hiring and promotion decisions to assess all candidates based on the same criteria.

- Implement anonymous resume reviews for initial candidate screening to reduce bias based on names, backgrounds, or affiliations.

- Multiple reviewers are required to assess promotion candidates independently before making final decisions.

Example:

A financial services firm implements anonymous resume reviews during the initial candidate screening process, removing names, universities, and other identifying information that could introduce bias. Hiring managers are provided only with skills, experience, and qualifications to evaluate candidates. As a result, the firm sees a 20 percent increase in diversity among candidates invited to interviews, leading to more inclusive hiring practices and a broader talent pool.

2. Standardize Hiring and Promotion Processes

A lack of clear, consistent policies often leads to biased decision-making. Establishing standardized procedures ensures fairness and objectivity.

Key Actions:

- Develop clear job descriptions focusing on required skills and competencies rather than subjective qualities.

- Use structured interview questions that assess candidates based on predetermined job-related criteria.

- Diversity hiring and promotion panels are required to ensure multiple perspectives are considered in decision-making.

- Document the reasoning behind hiring and promotion decisions to create transparency and accountability.

- Regularly review promotion data to identify patterns of inequity and take corrective action.

Example:

A healthcare organization adopts structured interview questions focusing solely on job-related competencies, such as technical skills, problem-solving, and cultural fit. This ensures that all candidates are evaluated based on the same criteria. Interview panels are trained to avoid personal biases and follow a consistent evaluation process for every candidate. This approach leads to fairer, more objective hiring decisions and reduces the impact of unconscious bias in the recruitment process.

3. Foster Transparent Communication in the Workplace

Open communication between employees and leadership builds trust and ensures employees understand how decisions are made.

Key Actions:

- Clearly communicate hiring and promotion criteria to all employees so they know what is expected for advancement.

- Provide employees with regular updates on organizational DEI initiatives, promotion data, and workforce diversity metrics.

- Establish town halls or open forums where employees can ask leadership questions about promotion policies and workplace equity efforts.

- Create anonymous reporting mechanisms where employees can express concerns about bias or unfair practices.

- Train managers on effective communication techniques that encourage openness, active listening, and constructive feedback.

Example:

A technology company establishes quarterly town halls where employees can directly ask leadership about promotion policies, career development opportunities, and ongoing workplace equity initiatives. During these open forums, leaders transparently discuss the company's progress, challenges, and plans for improving diversity and inclusion. This fosters a culture of trust and transparency, where employees feel empowered to voice concerns and understand how policies are evolving to support equity.

4. Ensure Equitable Access to Opportunities

Bias in decision-making often stems from unequal access to growth and leadership opportunities. Addressing these gaps can help mitigate bias.

Key Actions:

- Offer mentorship and sponsorship programs to help underrepresented employees gain visibility and career development opportunities.

- Ensure all employees have equal access to high-profile projects and leadership training programs.

- Regularly track and analyze participation in leadership development programs to ensure equitable representation.

- Encourage managers to recommend qualified employees from diverse backgrounds for promotion consideration proactively.

- Provide clear career pathway guidance to help employees understand how to advance within the organization.

Example:

A retail company encourages managers to proactively recommend qualified employees from diverse backgrounds for promotion by incorporating this into performance review processes and leadership development discussions. To build trust, the company holds regular meetings where managers are trained on unconscious bias, promoting inclusivity, and recognizing potential in employees from all backgrounds. This leads to more diverse talent being nominated for promotions, fostering an environment where employees feel supported and valued for their contributions.

5. Establish Mechanisms for Continuous Feedback and Improvement

Bias mitigation and transparent communication require ongoing assessment and adaptation.

Key Actions:

- Conduct regular employee surveys to measure perceptions of fairness and inclusivity in hiring and promotions.

- Hold structured feedback sessions where employees can discuss their experiences with workplace equity and advancement opportunities.

- Create a DEI advisory board with employees from different levels and backgrounds to review and refine workplace policies.

- Implement real-time feedback mechanisms where employees can share concerns about bias and receive timely responses from leadership.

- Require leadership teams to report on bias mitigation and transparency efforts as part of their annual performance evaluations.

Example:

A global marketing agency implements structured feedback sessions where employees can openly discuss their experiences with workplace equity, advancement opportunities, and any challenges they face in career progression. These sessions are held quarterly, and feedback is gathered anonymously to ensure employees feel comfortable sharing honest insights. The company uses the feedback to make data-driven adjustments to policies and practices, resulting in more equitable career growth opportunities for all employees.

Final Thoughts

Mitigating bias and fostering transparent communication are essential for building an equitable workplace where all employees feel valued and supported. By implementing this framework, organizations can create fairer decision-making processes, increase trust between employees and leadership, and establish a culture of accountability and inclusion.

Inclusive Leadership Development Framework

Purpose: Train leaders and managers to foster equitable workplace cultures by addressing bias, promoting inclusion, and supporting diverse talent. This framework provides a structured approach to developing inclusive leadership behaviors and creating an environment where all employees can thrive.

1. Build Self-Awareness and Self-Reflection

Leaders must first understand their biases and recognize how they influence decision-making, team dynamics, and workplace culture.

Key Actions:

- Conduct regular training on unconscious bias, microaggressions, and privilege awareness.

- Use self-assessment tools to help leaders identify and acknowledge personal biases.

- Create an open dialogue where employees can share their experiences with bias and exclusion.

- Encourage leaders to seek feedback from diverse team members to gain insight into their blind spots.

Example:

A health center CEO takes unconscious bias training and realizes their hiring patterns favor candidates from narrow backgrounds. They commit to expanding their talent pipeline to include HBCUs, Hispanic-Serving Institutions (HSIs), and community-based job programs.

2. Set Clear Expectations for Inclusive Leadership

Inclusion should be a core leadership competency, with clear expectations and accountability built into performance evaluations.

Key Actions:

- Define what inclusive leadership looks like, including active listening, empathy, equitable decision-making, and fostering diverse perspectives.

- Train leaders on inclusive communication skills, such as avoiding assumptions, validating employee experiences, and engaging in meaningful dialogue.

- Provide leadership coaching that focuses on inclusive behaviors and cultural competency.

- Recognize and reward leaders who demonstrate advocacy for fair policies and practices.

Example:

A COO receives DEI coaching after learning that diverse staff feel unheard, leading them to implement a Shared Voices

Initiative with structured team check-ins, rotating facilitators, and anonymous feedback tools. Within three months, staff engagement scores rise by 30 percent, turnover among underrepresented employees drops by 20 percent, and participation in leadership discussions increases. Seeing the success, the COO commits to ongoing coaching and inspires other leaders to adopt inclusive leadership practices, strengthening workplace culture and patient care.

4. Create a Culture of Belonging

Inclusive leaders create an environment where all employees feel valued, respected, and empowered to contribute.

Key Actions:

- Establish employee resource groups (ERGs) and affinity networks to support underrepresented employees and create voices for their ideas and perspectives.

- Promote psychological safety by ensuring employees feel comfortable speaking up without fear of retaliation through one-on-one meetings and anonymous feedback.

- Develop mentorship and sponsorship programs to support the career growth of diverse talent.

- Encourage leaders to celebrate cultural diversity through workplace initiatives and take time to understand the unique challenges different individuals face.

Example:

A clinic supervisor notices that some staff feel hesitant to speak in meetings. They implement a round-robin discussion method, ensuring that everyone can share insights.

3. Inclusive Decision-Making and Collaboration

Leaders are crucial in ensuring fairness in hiring, promotions, and project assignments. Decision-making processes must be transparent and free from bias.

Key Actions:

- Standardize interview and evaluation criteria to minimize subjective judgment.

- Diversity interview panels and hiring committees are required to increase fairness in candidate selection.

- Regularly review promotion and pay equity data to identify disparities and address systemic issues.

- Empower others by sharing leadership opportunities and responsibilities.

Example:

HR receives feedback that leadership roles lack diversity, so they implement a policy requiring diverse interview panels and hiring committees. The clinic sees an increase in diverse hires, with improved retention and engagement among under-represented staff. This shift leads to better patient-provider representation, enhancing trust and culturally competent care.

7. Commit to Continuous Learning and Advocacy

Inclusion is an ongoing process that requires continuous learning and adaptation as workplaces evolve.

Key Actions:

- Provide ongoing leadership training that evolves with emerging DEI challenges and best practices.

- Encourage leaders to stay informed on social and cultural issues that impact workplace dynamics.

- Foster cross-cultural learning by being a mentor and supporting individuals from underrepresented backgrounds.

- Encourage leaders to advocate for underrepresented employees by providing sponsorship and career development opportunities.

Example:

A CEO commits to fostering cross-cultural learning by mentoring emerging leaders from underrepresented backgrounds. Through structured mentorship and sponsorship, several mentees gain promotions into leadership roles, increasing diversity at the executive level. As a result, the organization benefits from more inclusive decision-making, improved employee morale, and stronger connections with diverse patient communities.

6. Hold Leaders Accountable for Inclusion Efforts

Sustained progress in workplace inclusion requires accountability at all levels of leadership.

Key Actions:

- Implement regular diversity, equity, and inclusion (DEI) assessments to measure leadership effectiveness in fostering inclusivity.

- Integrate inclusion-related goals into leadership performance reviews and feedback cycles, such as taking action to address systemic inequities.

- Tie inclusive leadership performance to executive and managerial compensation or incentive programs.

- Establish clear escalation pathways for employees to report concerns about bias or exclusionary behavior.

- Encourage peer accountability, where leaders hold each other responsible for upholding inclusive practices.

Example:

A management consulting firm implements annual DEI assessments to evaluate leadership effectiveness in fostering inclusivity, tying results to performance reviews. After the first assessment reveals gaps in staff belonging and equitable promotions, leaders must complete DEI training and action plans to address these issues. Within a year, employee engagement scores improved by 35 percent, promotions among underrepresented staff increased, and patient satisfaction rose, demonstrating stronger inclusivity at all levels.

▶ Final Thoughts

Developing inclusive leaders is not a one-time initiative but an ongoing commitment to fostering workplace equity, respect, and belonging. By following this framework, organizations can equip their leaders with the skills and mindset necessary to effectively create lasting change and support diverse talent.

Career Advancement and Empowerment Framework

Purpose: Support minority women in navigating corporate environments, developing their careers, and advocating for themselves through mentorship, training, networking, and leadership development. This framework provides a structured approach to overcoming career barriers and equipping minority women with the tools they need to succeed professionally.

1. Establish Clear Career Pathways

Lack of transparency in career advancement can create confusion and limit opportunities. Establishing clear pathways ensures employees understand what is required to progress in their careers.

- Work with HR and leadership to define career progression paths for different roles.

- Develop competency-based promotion criteria and communicate them clearly to employees.

- Provide self-assessment tools so employees can evaluate their skills and identify growth areas.

- Encourage employees to create individualized career development plans with measurable goals.

- Ensure that career advancement information is accessible, including through internal career coaching programs.

Example:

A software company develops competency-based promotion criteria, outlining specific skills, achievements, and leadership behaviors required for advancement. These criteria are clearly communicated through employee handbooks and quarterly team meetings. As a result, employees feel more empowered, and promotion requests rise, providing a more straightforward path to career advancement for all.

2. Build Strong Mentorship and Sponsorship Networks

Mentorship provides guidance and knowledge, while sponsorship ensures advocacy and career opportunities. Both are essential for professional growth.

- Create formal mentorship programs that pair minority women with senior leaders.

- Encourage cross-functional mentorship to expose employees to different aspects of the business.

- Develop sponsorship programs where senior executives actively advocate for high-potential employees.

- Provide mentorship training for senior employees to ensure effective and equitable support.

- Track and measure participation and success rates of mentorship programs to improve outcomes.

Example:

A consulting firm launches a sponsorship program where senior executives are paired with high-potential employees from underrepresented backgrounds. Executives actively advocate for these employees, providing opportunities for visibility, key projects, and leadership exposure. Sponsored employees are promoted to senior roles within a year, leading to increased diversity in leadership and stronger organizational performance.

3. Expand Access to Leadership Development Opportunities

Leadership training programs can help minority women gain the skills and confidence to advance into senior roles.

- Offer workshops on executive presence, negotiation skills, and strategic decision-making.

- Ensure leadership training programs are inclusive and accessible to diverse employees.

- Provide opportunities for minority women to take on stretch assignments and high-visibility projects.

- Encourage participation in external leadership development programs and industry conferences.

- Monitor leadership pipelines to ensure minority women are being prepared for senior roles.

Example:

A global marketing firm tracks its leadership pipeline to ensure minority women receive the necessary development opportunities for senior roles. They implement targeted leadership training programs, mentorship from senior executives, and clear career advancement metrics specifically for minority women. Within eighteen months, the number of minority women in senior leadership positions increases by 25 percent, strengthening diversity and representation at the executive level.

4. Strengthen Professional Networks and Visibility

Building strong networks is essential for career advancement and increasing access to opportunities.

- Facilitate networking events where minority women can connect with industry leaders and peers.

- Encourage participation in employee resource groups (ERGs) focused on career growth and leadership.

- Promote involvement in professional associations and industry groups.

- Provide guidance on effective networking strategies, including personal branding and LinkedIn optimization.

- Recognize and highlight the achievements of minority women in internal and external communications.

Example:

A tech company encourages employees to join employee resource groups (ERGs) focused on career growth and leadership development, making active participation a part of annual performance goals. ERG members gain access to exclusive mentorship, networking opportunities, and leadership training. As a result, engagement in ERGs increases, with participants reporting higher job satisfaction and an increase in promotions among ERG members.

5. Foster Self-Advocacy and Negotiation Skills

Equipping minority women with the ability to advocate for themselves is crucial for career progression.

- Offer training on salary negotiation, personal branding, and self-promotion.

- Encourage employees to document their accomplishments and contributions for performance reviews.

- Provide coaching on how to communicate career aspirations with managers.

- Teach strategies for navigating workplace challenges such as bias, microaggressions, and exclusion.

- Develop peer support groups where employees can share experiences and strategies for self-advocacy.

Example:

A corporate law firm offers training workshops on salary negotiation, personal branding, and employee self-promotion, especially targeting underrepresented groups. The program includes mock negotiation sessions, expert panels on building a personal brand, and strategies for advocating for career advancement. After the training, employees report a 50 percent increase in confidence when negotiating salaries, and within a year, promotion rates for underrepresented staff rise by 20 percent.

6. Measure and Track Career Advancement Progress

Tracking data and employee experiences ensures that career advancement efforts are effective and equitable.

- Collect and analyze promotion rates of minority women across different departments and levels.

- Regular employee surveys should be conducted to assess career satisfaction and perceived access to opportunities.

- Identify barriers preventing career progression and take corrective actions.

- Provide leadership with reports on the effectiveness of career development initiatives.

- Use insights from data to improve mentorship, training, and networking programs continuously.

Example:

A multinational corporation begins collecting and analyzing promotion rates of minority women across different departments and levels quarterly. By disaggregating the data by race, gender, and department, they identify discrepancies and implement targeted initiatives to address barriers to promotion, such as mentorship programs and leadership training. After one year, the company sees a 15 percent increase in the promotion rates of minority women, leading to more equitable representation at senior levels.

▶ Final Thoughts

Empowering minority women in the workplace requires a combination of clear career pathways, strong mentorship, leadership development, and self-advocacy. By implementing this framework, organizations can create an inclusive culture where all employees have the tools and support needed to succeed.

Unconscious Bias Awareness Exercise

Purpose:

The Unconscious Bias Awareness Exercise aims to help individuals recognize and understand the impact of unconscious bias in team meetings and workplace settings. Through scenario simulations, personal reflection, and group discussions, this tool aims to raise awareness of how biases can influence decision-making, communication, and collaboration. It encourages participants to develop strategies for mitigating bias and fostering more inclusive and equitable work environments.

This exercise promotes self-awareness and collaborative discussions on unconscious bias, helping participants recognize it in various situations and empowering them to make more equitable decisions.

Exercise: Unconscious Bias Awareness in Teams

Objective:

To help participants recognize their unconscious biases in workplace settings, particularly during team meetings, and understand how they can impact decision-making, communication, and collaboration.

Duration: 45 minutes

Materials Needed:

- A whiteboard or flip chart (or digital equivalent)
- Sticky notes or index cards
- Markers
- A timer

Step 1: Introduction to Unconscious Bias (10 minutes)

1. Brief Explanation: Start by defining unconscious bias:

   - Unconscious bias refers to the attitudes or stereotypes that unconsciously affect our understanding, actions, and decisions. These biases are formed over time based on cultural, social, and personal influences.

   - Bias can manifest in various forms, such as race, gender, age, ability, and socioeconomic status.

2. Examples in the Workplace:

   - Microaggressions: Subtle, unintentional actions that can be perceived as offensive or dismissive

   - Decision-making bias: How certain individuals may be favored or overlooked without clear reasons

   - Communication bias: How some people might dominate the conversation, or others may be overlooked in discussions

Step 2: Scenario Simulation (15 minutes)

1. Divide the Group: Split participants into small groups (3–4 people per group).

2. Scenario Creation: Provide each group with a different scenario that could occur in a team meeting or workplace setting. Here are a few examples:

   - A team meeting where one person consistently interrupts others

   - A situation where ideas from a female team member are overlooked, but a male colleague's idea is immediately accepted

   - A situation where someone from a different cultural background is not invited to contribute to a brainstorming session

   - A situation where an older team member is excluded from new technology discussions or a younger team member's experience is downplayed

3. Group Task: In each group, participants discuss how unconscious bias could affect the situation. They should consider:

   - Which biases could be affecting the people involved

   - How these biases impact the outcome of the situation (e.g., decision-making, communication, collaboration)

   - What behaviors or actions contribute to the bias

4. Debrief (Group Share): After 10 minutes of discussion, each group presents their scenario and thoughts. Write key points on the whiteboard or flip chart.

Step 3: Bias Recognition Reflection (10 minutes)

1. Personal Reflection: Ask participants to individually take 3–5 minutes to reflect on the following:

   - Have they ever witnessed or been part of a similar scenario in their team meetings?

   - How might their unconscious biases have impacted decisions or interactions in the past?

2. Self-Assessment: Provide participants with sticky notes or index cards to anonymously write down examples where they might have unintentionally displayed bias in meetings. Encourage participants to reflect on areas like:

   - Who do you tend to speak over or not acknowledge?

   - Who do you seek feedback from more often?

   - Whose ideas do you typically support or dismiss without considering them?

   - Collect the sticky notes, then read some out loud (without identifying who wrote them) to create a safe and reflective atmosphere.

Step 4: Group Action Plan (10 minutes)

1. Strategies to Mitigate Unconscious Bias: Encourage participants to brainstorm ways to combat unconscious bias in meetings. Write suggestions on the whiteboard. Some strategies may include:

   - Actively making space for quieter voices or diverse opinions

- Regularly reminding the team to seek input from everyone

- Having a "bias check" before decision-making (e.g., asking if everyone's ideas are being considered)

- Encouraging feedback on team dynamics and bias

2. Create Accountability: Discuss how the team can support one another in addressing unconscious bias. This might include:

   - Setting up a "bias buddy" system, where team members help each other recognize when bias is happening

   - Providing anonymous feedback channels to discuss any concerns about bias

3. Commitment: Have each participant write down one action they will take in their next team meeting to minimize bias and make meetings more inclusive.

Step 5: Closing Reflection (5 minutes)

1. Group Reflection: Ask participants how their perceptions of unconscious bias in meetings have changed and what they will do differently.

2. Final Thought: Remind participants that recognizing and addressing unconscious bias is ongoing. Encourage continued self-awareness and dialogue on the topic.

Privilege Self-Reflection Tool

Purpose Statement

This tool is designed to help individuals assess their privilege, identify areas of disadvantage, and recognize environments where they can be their authentic selves. This exercise encourages deeper self-awareness and intentional action by reflecting on different aspects of daily life—such as demographics, social settings, work, and healthcare. The goal is not to induce guilt or shame but to foster understanding, self-reflection, and informed decision-making about how one engages with the world and others.

Instructions

This tool is intended for personal growth, group discussions, or as part of a larger exploration of equity and self-awareness. It is a starting point for deeper conversations about privilege, identity, and creating inclusive spaces.

For each category, review the statements and mark:

- P (Privileged) if you benefit from advantages in this area

- U (Underprivileged) if you face barriers or disadvantages

- A (Authentic) where you feel comfortable being your true self

1. Demographics and Identity

Situation	P	U	A
My race/ethnicity is well represented in leadership roles.	☐	☐	☐
My gender identity does not limit my safety or opportunities.	☐	☐	☐
My sexual orientation does not impact my legal or social standing.	☐	☐	☐
My physical/mental abilities do not create barriers.	☐	☐	☐
My socioeconomic background provided financial stability.	☐	☐	☐
My religion (or lack of it) is widely accepted.	☐	☐	☐
I feel comfortable expressing my identity.	☐	☐	☐

2. Social Settings and Public Spaces

Situation	P	U	A
I feel safe and welcome in most social settings.	☐	☐	☐
I do not have to alter my behavior to fit in.	☐	☐	☐
I can access public restrooms and spaces without concern.	☐	☐	☐
I do not experience microaggressions or discrimination.	☐	☐	☐
I can express my views without fear of retaliation.	☐	☐	☐
I feel authentic in social settings.	☐	☐	☐

3. Grocery Stores and Daily Errands

Situation	P	U	A
I can easily find food/products that align with my needs.	☐	☐	☐
I do not feel monitored while shopping.	☐	☐	☐
I do not worry about the affordability of necessities.	☐	☐	☐
My local stores offer fresh, healthy options.	☐	☐	☐
I have reliable transportation for errands.	☐	☐	☐

4. Public Parks and Outdoor Spaces

Situation	P	U	A
I feel safe in public parks and recreation areas.	☐	☐	☐
I have access to well-maintained outdoor spaces.	☐	☐	☐
My community invests in green spaces.	☐	☐	☐
I can engage in outdoor activities without exclusion.	☐	☐	☐

5. Work and Career

Situation	P	U	A
My identity does not limit my job opportunities.	☐	☐	☐
I feel comfortable being authentic at work.	☐	☐	☐
I am paid fairly and have growth opportunities.	☐	☐	☐
My workplace supports diversity and inclusion.	☐	☐	☐
I do not experience bias or discrimination at work.	☐	☐	☐

6. Home and Family

Situation	P	U	A
I feel safe and supported in my home environment.	☐	☐	☐
My family accepts and respects my identity.	☐	☐	☐
I do not have to hide aspects of myself at home.	☐	☐	☐
I have stable housing and safe living conditions.	☐	☐	☐
I feel authentic and valued at home.	☐	☐	☐

7. Friends and Social Circles

Situation	P	U	A
My friends respect and affirm my identity.	☐	☐	☐
I do not have to hide aspects of myself.	☐	☐	☐
I feel comfortable setting boundaries.	☐	☐	☐
I do not experience exclusion or judgment.	☐	☐	☐
My social circle reflects my values.	☐	☐	☐

8. Healthcare and Well-Being

Situation	P	U	A
I have access to quality healthcare.	☐	☐	☐
I feel heard and respected by medical providers.	☐	☐	☐
I can afford the necessary medical treatments.	☐	☐	☐
I do not experience discrimination in medical settings.	☐	☐	☐
My health does not limit my opportunities.	☐	☐	☐

9. Social Determinants of Health (Community and Systems)

Situation	P	U	A
I live in a community with safe housing and clean air.	☐	☐	☐
I have access to high-quality education.	☐	☐	☐
My neighborhood has safe streets and reliable transit.	☐	☐	☐
I do not face systemic barriers to financial or legal support.	☐	☐	☐
My community promotes equity and social well-being.	☐	☐	☐

Reflection and Action Steps

After completing the tool, reflect on:

1. Identify Patterns

   - Look at where P, U, and A appear the most.

   - Are there areas where you experience privilege, but others do not?

   - Where do you feel most or least authentic?

2. Understand Your Identity

   - Which spaces make you feel comfortable and accepted?

   - Where do you feel the need to change aspects of yourself?

3. Take Action to Align with Your Values

- If privileged, how can you use your privilege to support others?

- If underprivileged, what steps can you take to access resources or support?

- If authenticity is lacking, how can you seek environments where you can be yourself?

ACKNOWLEDGMENTS

I owe much of my success to the blessings and teachings of my ancestors—especially my parents and grandparents—whose courage, confidence, and conviction have inspired me throughout my life. I would not have been able to complete this book without the invaluable help and support of my friends and family, particularly my husband. Their guidance, encouragement, and insights were indispensable, and I am deeply grateful for all their contributions.

I also want to express my heartfelt appreciation and gratitude to the fourteen women I interviewed. This research would not have been possible without your openness and passion for the topic. Your contributions inspired and motivated me in ways I will always cherish. Know that your voices will serve as a powerful source of guidance for women seeking career growth. I hope these eye-opening narratives will help advance the practice of truthlighting by encouraging honesty, clarity, and accountability in workplace conversations.

To expand the reach of my work, I felt compelled to convert my PhD dissertation, completed in 2023, into a book. This decision allowed me not only to share my research more broadly but also to reflect on my leadership legacy and the impact it can have on others. Revisiting my thesis revealed how much growth and learning I had experienced over the years, and it reinforced the desire to inspire others to pursue their paths. I hope each of you will take the time to reflect on your work and consider how it can be shared and expanded.

I was especially fortunate to have had Dr. Marianne Cabrera as my dissertation chair. Her unwavering support and commitment to my success helped me stay on track throughout this journey. Dr. Cabrera's ability to give me autonomy as a researcher while ensuring I adhered to sound ethical practices was crucial to the process. Thank you, Dr. Cabrera, for your patience and guidance and for making this experience enjoyable. I look forward to furthering this relationship in the years to come.

I also want to thank my fellow students in the cohort, my professors, and the editorial team (John C. Hawkins, Jason Shah, and Phyllis Crittenden) for their dedicated support. Special thanks to Dr. John Bennett for helping me navigate this dissertation's conceptual and theoretical framework and for sharing valuable references. I am grateful to my colleagues at work, my social justice practicum supervisor, Yerachmiel Ephraim (Rocky), and Dr. Ana McKee for providing vital support and resources throughout this project.

Writing a book based on my thesis was both easy and difficult. The ease came from already completing about 90 percent of the content, providing a strong foundation. However, the real challenge was ensuring that I maintained the integrity of the existing research while adapting it into a format accessible to a broader audience. The dense, academic language of the thesis required a shift toward a more reader-friendly style, all while preserving the depth of the findings. This balancing act was challenging but very rewarding. I am grateful to my editor and publisher, Chris O'Byrne, and my book coach, Meridith Eaton, for their invaluable guidance, thoughtful feedback, and steady support throughout this project.

For this book, I drew insights from my leadership experiences and the work of several influential thought leaders. One such voice was Deepa Purushothaman, whose book The First, The Few, and The Only offered valuable perspectives on leadership and diversity that enriched my understanding. I am deeply thankful for the endorsements of my esteemed readers, including Dr. Randall Pinkett, a scholar, researcher, and founder of BCT Partners, and Dr. Niru Kumar, a pioneer in DEI work in India. I would also like to extend my heartfelt appreciation to my dear friend Riikka Salonen, managing director of health equity at BCT Partners, for writing the foreword. Riikka is committed to DEI work, and I am honored by her support.

This book is dedicated to all women who aspire to grow professionally and achieve leadership roles, regardless of race, ethnicity, religious affiliation, culture, gender identity, sexual orientation, age, legal status, social status, or immigration status. The purpose of this book is to create awareness around the subtle, often unintentional actions that can amount to gaslighting—behaviors that sow doubt, diminish confidence, and undermine individuals' sense of reality. By bringing these patterns to light, this book aims to promote 'truthlighting'— a practice rooted in empathy, honesty, and validation that supports open dialogue, affirms lived experiences, and fosters trust in both personal and professional relationships. My goal is to motivate and inspire minority women to pursue their personal and professional goals despite the many challenges and barriers they face. My message to the next generation of women is this: Lead with humility, inspire with courage, guide with kindness, and succeed with determination.

REFERENCES

1. Graen, G. B., & Uhl-Bien, M. (1995).
    Development of leader-member exchange
    (LMX) theory of leadership over 25 years:
    Applying a multi-level multi-domain perspective.
    Leadership Quarterly, 6(2), 219-247. https://doi.
    org/10.1016/1048-9843(95)90036-5
2. Yukl, G. (2013). *Leadership in Organizations* (8th
    ed.), p. 224. Pearson Prentice Hall
3. Armenis, D. C., & Neal, A. (2008). Recognizing
    potential: A naturalistic investigation of employee
    promotion decisions. *Journal of Cognitive Engineering
    and Decision Making, 2*(1), 63–87. https://doi.
    org/10.1518/155534308X284372
4. Chernesky, R. H. (2003). Examining the glass
    ceiling: Gender influences on promotion decisions.
    Administration in Social Work, 27(2), 13-18.
    https://doi.org/10.1300/J147v27n02_02

5.   Gunatit Jyot. https://gunatitjyot.org
6.   Gerpott, F. H., Fasbender, U., & Burmeister, A. (2020). Respectful leadership and followers' knowledge sharing: A social mindfulness lens. *Human Relations*, 73(6), 789-810.
7.   Eurich, T. (2018). What self-awareness really is (and how to cultivate it). *Harvard Business Review*, 4(4), 1-9
8.   Ruderman, M. N., Ohlott, P. J., & Kram, K. E. (1995). Promotion decisions as a diversity practice. Journal of Management Development, 14(2), 6-23. https://doi.org/10.1108/02621719510078867
9.   De Brún, A., O'Donovan, R., & McAuliffe, E. (2019). Interventions to develop collectivistic leadership in healthcare settings: a systematic review. *BMC Health Services Research*, 19, 1-22
10. U.S. Bureau of Labor Statistics. (2024, January). *Women in the labor force: A Databook.* BLS Reports. https://www.bls.gov/opub/reports/womens-earnings/2022/home.htm
11. Siemiaticky, M. (2019). The diversity gap in the public-private partnership industry: An examination of women and visible minorities in senior leadership positions. *Annals of Public & Cooperative Economics, 90*(2), 393–414. https://doi.org/10.1111/apce.12240
12. McNeil, R. P. (2020). *Corporate Success: Exploring Promotions of Minority Women to GS-15 and Equivalent Government Positions* [Doctoral dissertation, Northcentral University]. https://www.proquest.com/openview/89ea501a96619ba72fc0104aeead8b04/1?pq-origsite=gscholar&cbl=18750&diss=y
13. Todak, N., Leban, L. & Hixon, B. (2021). Are women opting out? A mixed methods study of

women patrol officers' promotional aspirations. *Feminist Criminology, 16*, 658-679. https://doi.org/10.1177/15570851211004749

14. Alegria, S. (2019). Escalator or step stool? Gendered labor and token processes in tech work. *Gender & Society, 33*(5), 722–745. https://doi.org/10.1177/0891243219835737

15. Petersen, T., & Saporta, I. (2004). The opportunity structure for discrimination. American Journal of Sociology, 109(4), 852-901. https://doi.org/10.1086/378536

16. Chin, J. L. (2013). Diversity leadership: Influence of ethnicity, gender, and minority status. *Open Journal of Leadership, 2*(01), 1. http://doi.org/10.4236/ojl.2013.21001

17. Volini, E., Schwartz, J., Indranil. R., Hauptmann, M., Yves, D.V., Brad, D., & Bersin, J. (2019). *Leadership for the 21st century: The intersection of the traditional and the new.* Deloitte Insights. https://www2.deloitte.com/us/en/insights/focus/human-capital-trends/2019/21st-century-leadership-challenges-and-development.html

18. Ganesan, S., Weitz, B. A., & John, G. (1993). Hiring and promotion policies in sales force management: Some antecedents and consequences. *Journal of Personal Selling & Sales Management, 13*(2), 15-26. https://doi.org/10.1080/08853134.1993.10753944

19. McKinsey & Company. Women in the Workplace 2021. https://www.mckinsey.com/~/media/mckinsey/featured%20insights/diversity%20and%20inclusion/women%20in%20the%20workplace%202021/women-in-the-workplace-2021.pdf

20. McKinsey & Company. Women in the Workplace 2022. https://www.mckinsey.com/~/media/mckinsey/featured%20insights/diversity%20and%20inclusion/women%20in%20the%20workplace%202022/women-in-the-workplace-2022.pdf

21. Cortina, L. M., Kabat-Farr, D., Leskinen, E. A., Huerta, M., & Magley, V. J. (2013). Selective incivility as modern discrimination in organizations: Evidence and impact. *Journal of Management, 39*(6), 1579–1605. https://doi.org/10.1177/0149206311418835

22. U.S. Bureau of Labor Statistics. (2022, January 19). 2021 *Annual Averages – Household Data.* https://www.bls.gov/cps/aa2021/cpsaat09.pdf

23. Vazquez, A. H. (2021). *Individual and Cultural Influences on Occupational Stereotypes* (Order No. 29161889) [Doctoral dissertation, Long Island University]. ProQuest Dissertations & Theses Global: The Sciences and Engineering Collection. (2691072356). https://www.proquest.com/dissertations-theses/individual-cultural-influences-on-occupational/docview/2691072356/se-2

24. Tomkiewicz, J., Brenner, O. C., & Adeyemi-Bello, T. (1998). The impact of perceptions and stereotypes on the managerial mobility of African Americans. *The Journal of Social Psychology, 138*(1), 88–92. https://doi.org/10.1080/00224549809600356

25. Leswing, K. (2024, July 10). *Microsoft DEI leader says company is backing away from diversity commitments as internal team disbanded.* Business Insider. https://www.businessinsider.com/microsoft-layoffs-dei-leader-email-2024-7

26. McKinsey & Company. (2020). Diversity wins: How inclusion matters. https://www.mckinsey.com/business-functions/people-and-organizational-performance/our-insights/diversity-wins-how-inclusion-matters

27. BetterUp. (2021). The value of belonging at work: New frontiers for inclusion.

28. Delizonna, L. (2017, August 8). High-performing teams need psychological safety. Harvard Business Review.

29. Lorenzo, R., Voigt, N., Schetelig, K., Zawadzki, A., Welpe, I., & Brosi, P. (2018). How diverse leadership teams boost innovation. Boston Consulting Group. https://www.bcg.com/publications/2018/how-diverse-leadership-teams-boost-innovation

30. Hong, L., & Page, S. E. (2004). Groups of diverse problem solvers can outperform groups of high-ability problem solvers. Proceedings of the National Academy of Sciences, 101(46), 16385–16389. https://doi.org/10.1073/pnas.0403723101

31. Burns, C., Barton, K., & Kerby, S. (2012). The costly business of discrimination: The economic costs of discrimination and the financial benefits of gay and transgender equality in the workplace. Center for American Progress. https://www.americanprogress.org/article/the-costly-business-of-discrimination/

32. Bourke, J., & Dillon, B. (2018). The diversity and inclusion revolution: Eight powerful truths. *Deloitte Review, 22*(1), 83-92.

33. U.S. Equal Employment Opportunity Commission. (2021). EEOC releases fiscal year 2021 enforcement and litigation data.

34. Glassdoor. (2020). Diversity & inclusion workplace survey. https://www.glassdoor.com/blog/diversity-inclusion-workplace-survey/

35. Kirchmeyer, C. (1995). Demographic similarity to the work group: A longitudinal study of managers at the early career stage. *Journal of Organizational Behavior, 16*(1), 67-83. https://doi.org/10.1002/job.4030160109

36. Ryan, M. K., & Haslam, S. A. (2005). The glass cliff: Evidence that women are over-represented in precarious leadership positions. *British Journal of Management, 16*(2), 81–90. https://doi.org/10.1111/j.1467-8551.2005.00433.x

37. Cook, A., & Glass, C. (2014). Above the glass ceiling: When are women and racial/ethnic minorities promoted to CEO? *Strategic Management Journal, 35*(7), 1080-1089. https://doi.org/10.1002/smj.2161

38. Sapp, V. (2021). *African American Senior Executive Success Experiences in Fortune 500 Companies* [Doctoral dissertation, Concordia University Chicago]. https://www.proquest.com/openview/604140c6f8bf207a0ef7dd341beaf778/1?pq-origsite=gscholar&cbl=18750&diss=y

39. Shaughnessy, B. A., Treadway, D. C., Breland, J. A., Williams, L. V., & Brouer, R. L. (2011). Influence and promotability: The importance of female political skill. Journal of Managerial Psychology, 26(7), 584-603. https://doi.org/10.1108/02683941111164490

40. McClean, E. J., Martin, S. R., Emich, K. J. & Woodruff, T. (2018). The social consequences of voice: An examination of voice type and gender on status and subsequent leader emergence. *Academy of Management Journal, 61*(5), 1869-1891. https://doi.org/10.5465/amj.2016.0148

41. Crenshaw, K. (2017). *Kimberlé Crenshaw on intersectionality, more than two decades later.* Columbia Law School. https://www.law.columbia.edu/pt-br/news/2017/06/kimberle-crenshaw-intersectionality

42. Lazauskaitė-Zabielskė, J., & Bagdžiūnienė, D. (2008). The role of organizational justice in promotion decisions. *Psichologija, 38,* 46-82. https://doi.org/10.15388/Psichol.2008.0.2604

43. Beauchamp, T. L., & Childress, J. F. (2019). *Principles of Biomedical Ethics.* (4th ed.). Oxford University Press.

44. Baron, J. N., Davis-Blake, A., & Bielby, W. T. (1986). The structure of opportunity: How promotion ladders vary within and among organizations. *Administrative Science Quarterly, 31*(2), 248–273. https://doi.org/10.2307/2392790

45. Castilla, E. J. (2008). Gender, race, and meritocracy in organizational careers. *American Journal of Sociology, 113*(6), 1479–1526. https://doi.org/10.1086/588738

46. Beehr, T. A., & Taber, T. D. (1993). Perceived intra-organizational mobility: Reliable versus exceptional performance as means to getting ahead. *Journal of Organizational Behavior, 14*(6), 579–594. http://www.jstor.org/stable/2488109

47. Searle, R., & Skinner, D. (Eds.). (2011). Trust in the context of performance appraisal. In *Trust and human resource management.* p. 248. Edward Elgar Publishing. https://doi.org/10.4337/9780857932006

48. Khattab, J., van Knippenberg, D., Pieterse, A. N., & Hernandez, M. (2020). A network utilization perspective on the leadership advancement of minorities. The Academy of Management

Review, 45(1), 109-129. https://doi.org/10.5465/
amr.2015.0399

49. Cook, S. W. (1987). Behavior-change implications
of low involvement in an issue. Journal of
Social Issues, 43(1), 105-112. https://doi.
org/10.1111/j.1540-4560.1987.tb02336.x

50. Feagin, J. R. (1987). Changing Black Americans to fit
a racist system? Journal of Social Issues, 43(1), 85-89.
https://doi.org/10.1111/j.1540-4560.1987.tb02332.x

51. Yu, H. H. (2020). Revisiting the bamboo ceiling:
Perceptions from Asian Americans on experiencing
workplace discrimination. Asian American Journal of
Psychology, 11(3), 158-167. https://doi.org/10.1037/
aap0000193

52. Gustafsson, S., & Swart, J. (2020). 'It's not all it's
cracked up to be': Narratives of promotions in elite
professional careers. *Human Relations*, *73*(9), 1199-
1225. https://doi.org/10.1177/0018726719859404

53. Lemons, M. A., & Jones, C. A. (2001). Procedural
justice in promotion decisions: using perceptions of
fairness to build employee commitment. *Journal of
Managerial Psychology*, *16*(4), 268-281. https://doi.
org/10.1108/02683940110391517

54. Saal, F. E., & Moore, S. C. (1993). Perceptions
of promotion fairness and promotion candidates'
qualifications. *Journal of Applied Psychology*, *78*(1),
105. https://doi.org/10.1037/0021-9010.78.1.105

55. Colquitt, J. A., Conlon, D. E., Wesson, M. J.,
Porter, C. O., & Ng, K. Y. (2001). Justice at the
millennium: a meta-analytic review of 25 years of
organizational justice research. *Journal of Applied
Psychology*, *86*(3), 425. https://oce.ovid.com/
article/00004565-200106000-00006/HTML

56. Castilla, E. J. & Ranganathan, A. (2020). The production of merit: How managers understand and apply merit in the workplace. *Organization Science, 31*(4), 909-935. https://doi.org/10.1287/orsc.2019.1335

57. Taylor, M. *A. S. (2014). Armstrongs handbook of human resource management practice.* Kogan Page Limited.

58. Samuel, M. O., & Chipunza, C. (2009). Employee retention and turnover: Using motivational variables as a panacea. *African journal of business management, 3*(9), 410. https://academicjournals.org/article/article1380550130_Samuel%20and%20Chipunza%20pdf.pdf

59. Elmholdt, K., Elmholdt, C., Tanggaard, L., & Mersh, L. H. (2016). Learning good leadership: a matter of assessment? *Human Resource Development International, 19*(5), 406–428. https://doi.org/10.1080/13678868.2016.1206362

60. Church, A. H., Guidry, B. W., Dickey, J. A., & Scrivani, J. A. (2021). Is there potential in assessing for high potential? Evaluating the relationships between performance ratings, leadership assessment data, designated high-potential status and promotion outcomes in a global organization. The Leadership Quarterly, 32(5), 101516. https://doi.org/10.1016/j.leaqua.2021.101516

61. Harry, A. S., & Barinua, V. (2022). Workplace promotion system and employee attitude to work in access bank plc, Port Harcourt. *BW Academic Journal,* 22. https://www.bwjournal.org/index.php/bsjournal/article/view/679

62. Ballinger, G. A., & Schoorman, F. D. (2007). Individual reactions to leadership succession in workgroups. *Academy of Management Review, 32*(1), 118-136. https://doi.org/10.5465/amr.2007.23463887

63. Brodt, S. E., & Dionisi, A. M. (2011). When peers become leaders: The effects of internal promotion on workgroup dynamics. In *Trust and Human Resource Management*. Edward Elgar Publishing. https://doi.org/10.4337/9780857932006.00024

64. Tzafrir, S. S., & Hareli, S. (2009). Employees' emotional reactions to promotion decisions: The role of causal attributions and perceptions of justice. *Career Development International, 14*(4), 351-371. https://doi.org/10.1108/13620430910979844

65. Steel, R. P., & Landon, T.E. (2010). Internal employment opportunity and external employment opportunity: Independent or interactive retention effects? *Military Psychology, 22*(3), 282–300. https://doi.org/10.1080/08995605.2010.492692

66. Taylor, D. M., Moghaddam, F. M., Gamble, I., & Zellerer, E. (1987). Disadvantaged group responses to perceived inequality: from passive acceptance to collective action. *Journal of Social Psychology, 127*(3), 258.

67. Yu, D. & Liang, J. (2004). A new model for examining the leader-member exchange (LMX) theory. *Human Resource Development International, 7*(2), 251–264. https://doi.org/10.1080/1367886042000243826

68. Graen, G. B., & Scandura, T. A. (1987). Toward a psychology of dyadic organizing. *Research in*

Organizational Behavior, 9, 175–208. https://psycnet.
apa.org/record/1988-15584-001.

69. Liden, R. C., Sparrowe, R. T., & Wayne, S. J. (1997).
*Leader-member exchange theory: The past and potential
for the future.* (pp. 47-119). Elsevier Science/JAI Press.

70. Den Hartog, D. N., De Hoogh, A. H. B., &
Belschak, F. D. (2020). Toot your own horn? Leader
narcissism and the effectiveness of employee self-
promotion. *Journal of Management, 46*(2), 261–286.
https://doi.org/10.1177/0149206318785240

71. Borman, W. C., White, L. A., & Dorsey, D.
W. (1995). Effects of ratee task performance
and interpersonal factors on supervisor and
peer performance ratings. *Journal of Applied
Psychology, 80*(1), 168–177. https://doi.
org/10.1037/0021-9010.80.1.168

72. Alessandri, G., Cortina, J. M., Sheng, Z., &
Borgogni, L. (2021). Where you came from and
where you are going: The role of performance
trajectory in promotion decisions. *Journal of
Applied Psychology, 106*(4), 599–623. https://doi.
org/10.1037/apl0000696

73. Reb, J., & Greguras, G. J. (2010). Understanding
performance ratings: Dynamic performance,
attributions, and rating purpose. *Journal of Applied
Psychology, 95*(1), 213–220. https://doi.org/10.1037/
a0017237

74. Powell, G. N., & Butterfield, D. A. (2002).
Exploring the influence of decision makers' race and
gender on actual promotions to top management.
Personnel Psychology, 55(2), 397-428. https://doi.
org/10.1111/j.1744-6570.2002.tb00115.x

75. Breaugh, J. A. (2011). Modeling the managerial promotion process. Journal of Managerial Psychology, 26(4), 264-277. https://doi.org/10.1108/02683941111124818

76. Furnham, A., & Petrides, K. V. (2006). Deciding on promotions and redundancies: Promoting people by ability, experience, gender, and motivation. *Journal of Managerial Psychology, 21*(1), 6–18. https://doi.org/10.1108/02683940610643189

77. Lockamy, A. I., & Service, R. W. (2011). Modeling managerial promotion decisions using Bayesian networks: An exploratory study. Journal of Management Development, 30(4), 381-401. https://doi.org/10.1108/02621711111126846

78. Porter, D. M. (2001). Gender differences in managers' conceptions and perceptions of commitment to the organization. *Sex Roles, 45*(5/6), 375-398. https://link.springer.com/content/pdf/10.1023/A:1014313732152.pdf

79. Higgins, C. A., Judge, T. A., & Ferris, G. R. (2003). Influence tactics and work outcomes: A meta-analysis. *Journal of Organizational Behavior: The International Journal of Industrial, Occupational and Organizational Psychology and Behavior, 24*(1), 89-106. https://doi.org/10.1002/job.181

80. Ferris, G., Davidson, S., & Perrewe, P. (2005). p. 127. *Political skill at work: impact on work effectiveness.* Davies.

81. Crawshaw, J. R. (2011). Career development, progression, and trust. *In Trust and Human Resource Management. Edward Elgar Publishing.* https://doi.org/10.4337/9780857932006.00018

82. Feldman, D. C., & Weitz, B. A. (1991). From the invisible hand to the gladhand: Understanding a careerist orientation to work. *Human Resource Management, 30*(2), 237-257. https://doi.org/10.1002/hrm.3930300206

83. Grandison, T., & Sloman, M. (2000). A survey of trust in internet applications. *IEEE Communications Surveys & Tutorials, 3*(4), 2-16. https://doi.org/10.1109/COMST.2000.5340804

84. Mayer, R. C., Davis, J. H., & Schoorman, F. D. (1995). An integrative model of organizational trust. *Academy of Management Review, 20*(3), 709-734. https://doi.org/10.2307/258792.

85. Brockner, J., & Siegel, P. (1996). Understanding the interaction between procedural and distributive justice: The role of trust. In R. E., Kramer, R. M., & Tyler, T. R. (Eds), *Trust in organizations: Frontiers of theory and research* (pp. 390-413). SAGE Publications, Inc. https://doi.org/10.4135/9781452243610

86. Wang, Q., Wang, A., & Li, R. (2019). The impact of promotion justice on job performance and organizational citizenship behavior: The mediating role of trust. Paper presented at the *2019 3rd International Seminar on Education, Management and Social Sciences (ISEMSS 2019)*, 121-125. https://doi.org/10.2991/isemss-19.2019.21

87. Whitener, E. M., Brodt, S. E., Korsgaard, M. A., & Werner, J. M. (1998). Managers as initiators of trust: An exchange relationship framework for understanding managerial trustworthy behavior. *Academy of Management Review, 23*(3), 513-530. https://doi.org/10.2307/259292.

88. Blau, P. M. (1964). Justice in social exchange. *Sociological Inquiry, 34*(2), 193-206. https://doi. org/10.1111/j.1475-682X.1964.tb00583.x

89. Mayer, R. C., & Davis, J. H. (1999). The effect of the performance appraisal system on trust for management: A field quasi-experiment. *Journal of Applied Psychology, 84*(1), 123-136. https://psycnet.apa.org/buy/1999-10108-010.

90. Dwyer-Owens, D. (2015). *Values, Inc.: How incorporating values into business and life can change the world.* Beacon Publishing.

Additional references utilized in the thesis are not necessarily paired with the footnote.

Beehr, T. A., Nair, V. N., Gudanowski, D. M., & Such, M. (2004). Perceptions of reasons for promotion of self and others. *Human Relations, 57*(4), 413-438. https://doi.org/10.1177/0018726704043894

Cahn, N. (n.d.). *Women's status and pay in C-suite: New Study.* Forbes. https://www.forbes.com/sites/naomicahn/2021/02/19/womens-status-and-pay-in-the-c-suite--new-study/?sh=159080737621

Fiske, S. T. (1987). On the road: Comment on the cognitive stereotyping literature on Pettigrew and Martin. Journal of Social Issues, 43(1), 113-118. https://doi.org/10.1111/j.1540-4560.1987.tb02337.x

Indeed. (n.d.). *A guide to salaried employees: Everything to know about hours, overtime and more.* https://www.indeed.com/hire/c/info/salaried-employees-guide#:~:text=According%20to%20the%20Fair%20Labor%20Standards%20Act%2C%20

a,aren%E2%80%99t%20entitled%20to%20
overtime%20or%20a%20minimum%20wage

Marshall, D. A. (2022). Changes executives need to implement to promote women to executive positions. *Dissertation Abstracts International, 83*(4-A).

Mills, A. J., Durepos, G., & Wiebe, E. (2010). Credibility. *Encyclopedia of case study research* (Vols. 1-0). SAGE Publications, Inc. https://doi.org/10.4135/9781412957397

Murray, C. (2014). *A qualitative study on minority men and women's perceived barriers to senior executive service advancement* (Order No. 3647300) [Doctoral dissertation, University of Phoenix]. ProQuest Dissertations and Theses Global: Business. (1630026811). https://www.proquest.com/openview/e30c19accabeb9f1c058d611ea57cac3/1?pq-origsite=gscholar&cbl=18750

Polit, D.F., & Beck, C.T. (2012). *Nursing research: Generating and assessing evidence for* nursing practice. Lippincott Williams and Wilkins.

Son Hing, L. S., Bobocel, D. R., Zanna, M. P., Garcia, D. M., Gee, S. S., & Orazietti, K. (2011). The merit of meritocracy. *Journal of Personality and Social Psychology, 101*(3), 433 – 450. https://doi.org/10.1037/a0024618

Merriam-Webster. (n.d.). Advocate. In *Merriam-Webster.com dictionary*. Retrieved April 13, 2020, from https://www.merriam-webster.com/dictionary/advocate

INDEX

E

F

ABOUT THE AUTHOR

Dr. Falguni Shah immigrated to the United States from Mumbai, India, in 2001, guided by a deep sense of purpose, big dreams, and a lifelong commitment to learning and service. She holds a PhD in Organizational Leadership from Adler University, a Master's degree in Community Counseling from Loyola University Chicago, and a Bachelor's degree in Medicine and Surgery from the University of Mumbai.

With over two decades of experience in healthcare, Dr. Shah brings a distinctive blend of clinical expertise, technical skills, business acumen, systems thinking, and cultural humility to her work. Her career spans leadership roles in federally qualified health centers and community mental health, with a focus on healthcare quality, compliance, and accreditation. As a speaker and consultant, Dr. Shah delivers leadership coaching, equips leaders to guide diverse teams, builds inclusive leadership competencies, and sparks awareness around implicit bias. She helps organizations strengthen workforce systems and create cultures where people thrive.

Grounded in spiritual values and a deep belief in the dignity of every human being, Dr. Shah is passionate about justice and equality. She cares deeply about wellness and enjoys travelling and exploring new cultures. Rooted in both Eastern values and Western traditions, she brings heart, perspective, and purpose to every space she enters.